ANCIENT
AFRICAN
KINGDOMS

ANCIENT
AFRICAN
KINGDOMS

by Margaret Shinnie

LONDON
EDWARD ARNOLD (PUBLISHERS) LTD

PRINTED IN GREAT BRITAIN BY
FLETCHER AND SON LTD, NORWICH
8919/64

Contents

Preface

SOME years ago, a young African archaeologist, graduate of an African University, told me that while he had been taught little of the geography of his country and continent, he had had to learn that of London intimately, and that one of the questions set in a geography paper at some stage of his career had invited him to show how to reach the suburb of Hampstead from Blackfriars Bridge by underground train. More recently, the study of Africa in all its aspects has been intensified, many textbooks have appeared, and African Universities and their students now naturally demand that much of what is taught should be African in content.

This book is intended to help in this, and gives an outline of the history of various states in Africa before the arrival of Europeans. It combines the work of archaeologist and historian, and seeks to avoid giving information which is still controversial. It is meant for those who have yet to decide on a career, in the hope that some of them may be sufficiently interested to wish to pursue the exploration of ancient Africa further. In reading this book they will see how much is still to be discovered, and perhaps they will feel something of the excitement which comes from fitting a newly found piece of information on to that which is already known.

Many people have helped me to write this book, and to all of them I offer my thanks, but I am particularly grateful to the people who took the trouble to read the manuscript and make valuable and interesting comments on it, Professor Anene, of the University of Ibadan; Dr G. S. P. Freeman-Grenville, of the Institute of African Studies, University of Ghana; and Dr and Mrs John Sharman, of Nairobi. My husband, Professor P. L. Shinnie, has helped me at every stage in the preparation of this book, and has allowed me to use his photographs – those which are not otherwise acknowledged are all his.

Head of a Queen Mother from Benin
(*Photo: Herbert List*)

1. 'The Land Shadowing With Wings'

IN the Bible, in the Book of the Prophet Isaiah, Africa is described as 'the land shadowing with wings' which lay beyond Ethiopia for it was unknown and untravelled at this time; while the existence of the continent was realised, its extent and all knowledge of it was hidden in mists and shadows from all the world except the Africans who lived there. For centuries it seemed dark with mystery to Europeans and other non-Africans, and the rumours which were spread were full of fantastic stories which peopled the land with tribes of giants and dwarfs, of people whose heads grew from under their arms, of monstrous animals, of inland seas, of magic, of gold and unimaginable wealth to be had for the finding.

These creatures were thought to inhabit Africa. From a medieval map.

Of course the coastal towns of Africa have been known and used by traders for at least as long as we have written history, especially those on the North African coast, along the Mediterranean Sea, and in the East, down the Red Sea and on the edges of the Indian Ocean; and recently historians have discovered that the Phoenicians traded round the Northwest coast too. We know these things because they are written down in ancient writings, those of ancient Egypt and particularly those of the Greek and Roman historians. Herodotus, a Greek, wrote in his *Histories* about North Africa and ancient Egypt, where he lived for a time in the fifth century B.C. He gives us some interesting information about Meroë, the capital of the ancient kingdom of Kush to the south of Egypt, though he did not go there, and his report is certainly based on hearsay. North Africa, the stretch of land covering those countries which we now know as Algeria, Tunisia, and Libya, was an important part of the Roman Empire, as many magnificent ruins testify. In exchange for their civilizing influences, the Romans took grain, slaves and wild animals for their arenas. Many Roman writers tell of events in North Africa, where Carthage is probably the name most familiar to us all. Conditions on the East Coast are described

A rock drawing of a giraffe from the Sahara—an animal which now only exists much further south.

9

The Roman town of Djemila in Algeria.

A desert caravan.

in a book called *The Periplus of the Erythraean Sea* written about A.D. 110 by a Greek for the use of sailors and traders using the ports and harbours there. Apart from nautical detail about winds, tides and harbours, he lists the kind of goods which might be well received by the coast dwellers, and what might be acquired in exchange. Later, Arab travellers and scholars and then Portuguese keep us informed of events in many parts of Africa, but of the inland peoples of this vast continent we hear very little, and then only rumour and speculation.

An 'Association for Promoting the Discovery of the Interior Parts of Africa' was set up in the eighteenth century in London, and with its help brave men of various nationalities set off on voyages of discovery. These journeys were full of danger, no more from the strange people the travellers would meet than from the difficulties of the climate they would have to endure. Africa is a continent of amazing contrasts. Geographically, it has almost every kind of land one can think of – arid desert in the Sahara and Kalahari; dense damp tropical forest in Central Africa; swamps near some coasts, and the *sudd* in the southern Sudan – a mass of tangled, reed covered, floating islands in the Nile; vast stretches of savannah land on the borders of deserts, with long 'elephant grass' and low trees and bushes; fertile soil and meadow lands in parts of South Africa and Rhodesia, and in Kenya and Uganda; mountains, great rivers, and lakes as large as seas; even snow near the Equator, on the peak of mount Kilimanjaro. When this incredible fact was first reported in England, in 1848, by one of the earliest missionaries, Johann Rebmann, it was treated with great scorn. Rebmann was told he could have seen only glistening white rock, but of course he was right, and a few years later a colleague reported snow on a second peak as well, that of Mount Kenya.

Climatically, the contrasts are just as great. The northern and southern extremes of the continent enjoy a temperate climate, with hot summers and warm winters, and enough rainfall to make crop growing profitable. The savannah lands are hot and dusty, often too dry for farming to be possible, though there is grass for the herds of cattle which nomads tend and rear there. The deserts are dry, going for years without rain, burning by day, and often, particularly in winter, bitterly cold by night. The forests are damp and misty, with heavy, almost daily, rainfall and thunderstorms, and virtually no change in temperature, day or night, winter or summer.

11

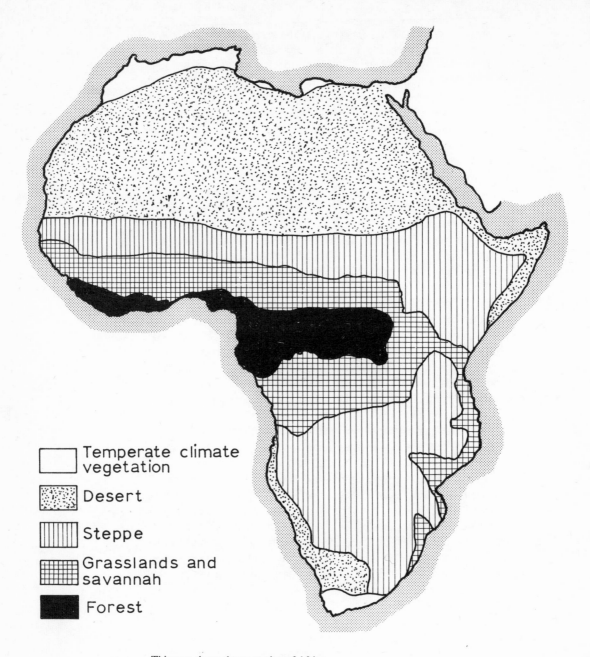

Temperate climate vegetation

Desert

Steppe

Grasslands and savannah

Forest

This map shows the vegetation of Africa.

These factors of climate and geography are important for the history of Africa, and neither is thought to have changed very much in *historic* times, that is to say during the times for which we have written history. The deserts have spread a little into more fruitful land and there is reason to believe that they were once themselves less arid, for Roman mosaics in North Africa and rock drawings in the Sahara show pictures of animals which could not now survive in those places, as do rock drawings in the northern Sudan, along the Nile. But it is unlikely that there has been enough change to make any real difference to the lives of Africans.

They have been greatly affected, however, by other factors; by disease in the malarial swamps; by the need for the cattle owners of the savannah to be perpetually on the move in search of pasture, which led to ceaseless strife about the ownership of land, and endless migrations; by the difficulty of penetrating the tropical forests, which meant that the people who lived there found it almost impossible to enjoy cultural contacts with other peoples; by the impassibility of the *sudd* which shut out the civilization of Egypt from the lands further south, with which contact would surely otherwise have been made along the River Nile. Nero, the Roman Emperor, sent two of his centurions with an expedition to

The Sudd in the Southern Sudan. The thin white line at the top of the picture is the river which has been mechanically cleared for river traffic. (*B.O.A.C.*)

penetrate 'Ethiopia' (as the Sudan was then called) and they reported that they were baulked by a huge swamp (the *sudd*) which prevented them from reaching the 'interior'.

But the greatest barrier of all must always have been the Sahara Desert, a hot, inhospitable expanse of sand making the most severe demands on all who would cross it, let alone those who tried to live there. It has been crossed, of course, at all times of human history; by caravans for trading purposes; by nomad tribes such as the Tuareg and Tebu; and by armies. Such journeys have never been lightly undertaken, however, for desert life makes such unusual demands on human endurance, calling for strict discipline and dedication to the work on hand, that they have always been regarded as a most serious undertaking, which might well meet with disaster. For this reason, many African states south of the Sahara had little contact with European, particularly Mediterranean, civilizations and developed in their own way their own forms of government and administration, their own art, and learned all the crafts and skills which enabled them to live and prosper.

Of the lands south of the Sahara, except for the East Coast, modern scholars know little before the arrival of the Europeans during the nineteenth century, for Africans kept no written records of events in their countries. In many countries, we are able to find out what went on in ancient times by reading records which were kept sometimes on stone, sometimes on clay or pottery, sometimes on scrolls of paper, metal, or even leather. But Africans, except for the Kushites, had no knowledge of writing, and in addition, little of their material culture is preserved; by this, we mean the things which they made and used, their tools, buildings, pottery, and weapons, for example. Of the ancient kingdoms which we shall study in this book, that of Kush alone produces a fine array of objects for us to see, and that is due at least partly to the luck of its position in a dry desert area where things buried in the ground are well preserved. Elsewhere, damp climates and white ants must have destroyed much that would otherwise have been found, so that in many cases all that is left of an ancient people for scientists to study are pottery and stone tools which are not much affected by climate.

Instead of written records, many African peoples kept in their memories the stories of their own people which were repeated by father to son down the generations and are remembered even to-

Examples of ancient writings used in other countries: Cuneiform from Mesopotamia, Egyptian hieroglyphs, Minoan script from Crete.

14

day. These stories form a sort of historical record. This is called 'oral tradition' by modern historians, and makes a valuable contribution to the study of African history, provided always that it is treated as a story and not as an exact record of actual events. In fact some of the stories are so fantastic that we should be most unlikely to believe in their literal truth, but even these frequently are based on true events. We shall see how oral tradition is used in later chapters.

Little by little, the history of Africa is being discovered, but there are still huge gaps in our knowledge, and with the patient work of historians and archaeologists much more will be found out. The historian searches through any records he can find, including those of other countries, to see if he can find any mention or description of Africa in them, and takes note of oral tradition. The archaeologist digs up places which were, for example, towns or temples, mines or workshops in ancient times; he studies the places he finds and the things buried in them, the tools, weapons, art, pottery, buildings or any other object which presents itself, comparing them with those of other cultures or other excavations. Year by year our knowledge of ancient Africa increases because of the work of these scholars, African and European, but over such a huge continent there will be work for generations of scholars for many years to come.

In the following chapters, we shall look at the development of a number of African states. They have been selected because they are ones which have been studied by scholars, and so we have come to know something of their history. A second reason is that they are spread over Africa and we can see what happened in different parts of the continent. Egypt and the countries of the North African coast have been left out altogether, because they were so much a part of the Mediterranean world that their development was quite different from that of the truly African kingdoms. But first of all, we shall look at a time when there were no states or boundaries, no different peoples or tribes, at a time when the world was young and man, as we know him, did not yet exist.

2. *Early Man*

ALTHOUGH we know comparatively little of its history, there is one field in which Africa has made a great contribution to knowledge. This is in the study of the origins of man, for in Africa there has been found a unique collection of the bones of the earliest beings, through which man's development can be traced. It is generally thought nowadays that man and ape, millions of years ago, both gradually developed from the same ape-like creature. The common idea that man was descended from apes is shown to be wrong by scientists who have studied the ancient bones which have been found. Even so, the earliest men were very ape-like, with the difference that they walked upright on two legs, had developed larger brains, and their jaws and teeth were much more like modern man's than like an ape's. With his larger brain, man was able to think and have ideas, and he began to use not only his brain, but also his hands for simple skills such as making stone tools. The ape-like creature, though he still looked more like a gorilla than like one of us, had become a thinking man.

Examples of the skulls of all these beings have been found in Africa, the earliest being those of ape-like creatures, possibly man's own ancestors, which were found on the eastern side of Lake Victoria. One of the most complete of these was nicknamed 'Proconsul' and although his exact age is not known, he may be as much as thirty million years old. So thrilled was the world at the discovery of man's earliest ancestor, that Proconsul was flown to London for study at the invitation of a big airline, given a seat to himself, and all the airports on his route were cleared so that when he landed there should be no risk of damage to his precious bones. Were we able to see Proconsul as he was when alive, we should certainly judge him to be an ape, but the formation of his bones makes it clear that in some respects he was quite different (as for example the length of his leg from knee to ankle which is longer than an ape's leg in proportion to his body). For this reason he is

A fossilized caterpillar from Olduvai of the period of Proconsul.

16

An imaginative drawing of Proconsul as he may have looked, based on a study of his bones. (*British Museum.*)

Man's first tools, looking like broken pebbles. This one is from Olduvai.

Hand axe.

Cleaver. These two both belong to the Old Stone Age.

thought to be an example of the ancient creature from whom man ultimately developed.

A more man-like creature than Proconsul was found in the Transvaal, and others like him in other parts of South Africa. He has been named 'Australopithecus' – a long word which only means 'southern ape' – and he may have lived 750,000 years ago. He had an ape-like face, but a bigger brain than any known ape, walked upright, as can be told from the formation of his bones, and had a more or less human jaw and teeth.

The first example of a being which could really be called Man was found at Olduvai in Tanganyika in 1959, by Dr Leakey, who is famous for his work on early man, and who also found Proconsul. This first man was nicknamed 'Nutcracker Man' by Dr Leakey, because of the obvious strength of his jaws, and though he must still have looked very much like an ape, he is considered to be a man because he made stone tools. These were of the simplest possible kind, but they were certainly tools and he had worked out the idea of making and using them. To us, who have a fine array of tools to help us in our daily lives, this may seem a very simple skill to have acquired, but it was an amazing advance, for it marks the development of man from pre-man. For the first time there was a brain which had ideas, realized how to carry out an idea, and controlled the hands which put it to practical use. 'Nutcracker Man' may be 600,000 years old, and there was a long way to go before man would look really human.

After Nutcracker Man, and from about half a million years ago, it is clear that people roamed all over Africa in search of food, leaving, as evidence of their passage, stone tools and bones. All over the continent, except in the central forest area, rather clumsy, pear-shaped stone tools are found, which are called 'hand axes'. They have been chipped into shape, always the same general shape, rounded at the thicker end, which was the working end, and tapering to a not very fine point at the thinner end, which was held in the hand. They are called 'hand' axes because it is assumed that they were held in the hand, and were used for a variety of purposes, mainly connected with food gathering. It is difficult for us to believe that, with such a clumsy implement for his only tool and weapon, early man could manage to survive, especially when one thinks of Africa's wild animals. To test the usefulness of the hand axe, and also to find out exactly what it could be made to do,

Dr Leakey, whom we have mentioned above, went out into the bush in Kenya, armed only with a hand axe, and lived for a period as early man must have done. He found that he was able to live, certainly not comfortably, but quite safely, and that he could kill and skin animals and so feed and clothe himself. He also used the hand axe for digging out of the ground roots which he could eat to vary his food. He found that he need have no fear of hunger, and could provide himself with warmth if he felt cold by wrapping himself in animal skins. It was an interesting and valuable experiment – probably very few of us would care to repeat it ourselves!

This period in the development of man is called the Old Stone or Paleolithic Age – which means exactly the same thing using Greek words – and it occurs all over Europe, and in many parts of Asia. We have found the greatest number of stone tools in Africa, and this seems to have been the centre of the people using hand axes. It seems most likely, therefore, that in these early times Africa led the way and was in the forefront during the earliest periods of man's development. It has been called 'the cradle of man', and it may well have been here that man first became man.

Above: Rock drawings from South Africa. Spearing fish from boats or floats.
Below: Shooting birds with a bow and arrow; the bag on the huntsman's back contains birds.

THE NEW STONE AGE

Up till the end of the Old Stone Age, man had been concerned with *collecting* his food, either by hunting and killing animals, or by digging in the ground for roots, or by picking wild fruits and berries. He had not discovered how to grow crops or to use animals; he was a hunter, not a farmer.

About 8,000 B.C., man discovered agriculture. Western Asia is known to be the home of the earliest crop growing and herding of domestic animals. The practice of agriculture goes hand in hand with the New Stone Age, or Neolithic period of pre-history in many places, and reached different areas at different times, so much so that some of the really primitive people in the world, such as the Australian Aborigines, had not progressed beyond Old Stone Age methods of food collecting until very recent times. The characteristic feature of the New Stone Age is the variety of stone tools which were made, many of them small and fine, and for purposes beyond those of merely killing and skinning animals. Many of these were chipped into shape, as in the Old Stone Age, but a

19

new skill was also employed, that of polishing stone. The polished stone axe is an implement which is found all over Africa.

Learning to farm was perhaps the most important advance which man ever made. One very obvious result was that his food was comparatively sure, but there were other effects as well. Once a man cultivated a piece of land, he regarded it and the crops he grew on it as his own, so that ideas of property and ownership began to arise. He settled on his piece of land, ceasing to wander in search of food, and so communities began to grow; and with his settled life, certainty of food, and greater leisure, he began to experiment in other crafts and learned to make pottery and baskets, simple houses and enclosures for his herds, rough cloth, and the tools of stone and bone which are so typical of this stage of his development. This sort of civilization spread from Western Asia into Europe and North Africa, and is clearly seen in Egypt, for example, at sites such as that in the Faiyum. Elsewhere in Africa,

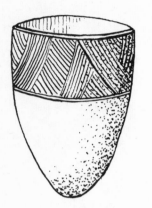

A neolithic cup from Hyrax Hill.

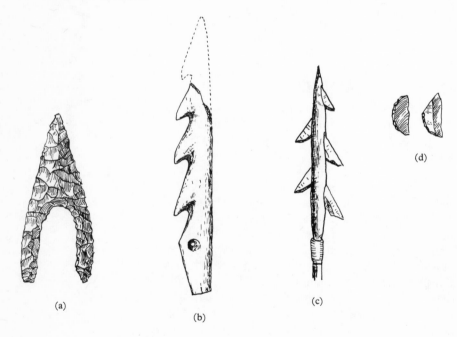

(a)

(b)

(c)

(d)

Examples of neolithic tools: (a) an arrow head from the Faiyum (b) a bone harpoon from Esh Shaheinab. A barbed arrow head (c) which is made of small stone implements (d) fitted into a wooden haft.

however, the development of agriculture was different, and appears to have been slower, because although we find pottery and stone tools typical of a Neolithic stage of progress, we find no evidence of agricultural pursuits. At Esh Shaheinab in the Sudan, tools and pottery were of Neolithic type, but there was no evidence of agricultural work and only the smallest indication of the domestication of animals; and Hyrax Hill, in Kenya, is similar. But the discovery of querns, used for grinding grain, at other Neolithic sites in Kenya, such as Nakuru and Njoro River caves suggests that some form of grain crop was produced here. In other parts of Africa, it is possible that root crops were cultivated, but there is no certain evidence for this, nor anything to show that animals were domesticated until much later times. Over much of the southern part of Africa, as far as we can tell at present, man remained a hunter and food collector, rather than becoming a farmer, though he used tools which were greatly superior to the hand axes of his forefathers.

With the experiments that he was making, man came to learn the use of metals, the mining, smelting, and working of copper and iron, which again was a great advance. As the use of metal reached a given area, so the Neolithic period came to an end, and the kingdoms of which we shall read in this book all belong to the times when metal was in use and man had reached a stage of development well in advance of the users of stone tools.

A polished stone axe, front and side view.

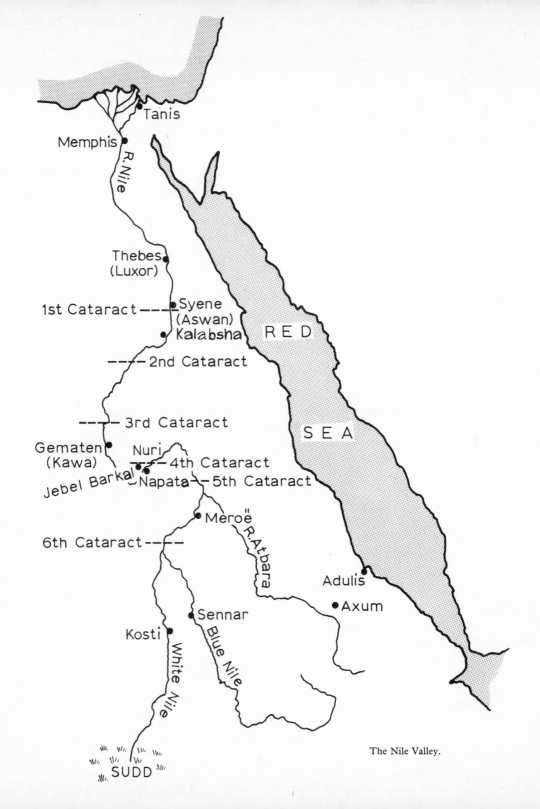

The Nile Valley.

3. *Kush*

KUSH is the name that was given by the ancient Egyptians to the kingdom which lay to the south of their borders. This kingdom became really important in the time of the Meroitic people, and was the most ancient of the independent kingdoms of Africa. It spread over a part of the country which we now know as the Republic of the Sudan, to the south of Egypt, and like Egypt, it has always been dependent on the great river Nile for its life.

From about 2000 B.C. the history of this part of Africa was closely linked with that of Egypt. At times it was actually a province of Egypt, though not further south than the fourth cataract, which was the southernmost boundary of Egyptian occupation. This occupation was not unbroken, for the Egyptians had troubles at home and periodically withdrew to their own land to cope with dangers which threatened them, (such as invasion by the Libyans, or internal struggles for power). But it was sufficiently continuous for there to be a marked Egyptian influence over the whole area, and many Egyptian towns and temples still stand along the banks of the Nile which must have been built and inhabited by Egyptian craftsmen, priests, administrators, and others. There was much trade between Egypt proper and the province of Kush, and at some time before 1100 B.C. an important religious centre of the Egyptian god Amun-Ra was built round a holy hill called Jebel Barkal, looking across the River Nile to the town of Napata. In Egyptian times, Napata was a big administrative centre, and was to become the first capital of the independent kingdom of Kush.

About 1100 B.C., the Egyptian empire began to decay, and we do not know what was happening in Kush, though it seems certain that Egyptian influence was still strong. So, precisely how it was that a Kushite king, called Kashta, came to decide that Kush was strong enough not merely to make itself independent of Egypt, but actually to conquer its former masters, is not known. He invaded

Part of a gold necklace of the period when Egyptian influence was very strong. (*Sudan Museum.*)

and conquered Egypt, and ruled over that country as far north as Thebes, the capital of Upper Egypt. This happened about 700 B.C., and not very long afterwards Kashta's son, Piankhy, completed the conquest of Egypt, and so became ruler of a land which stretched from the shores of the Mediterranean to the borders of modern Ethiopia – almost a quarter of the African continent. The Kushite kings settled down to enjoy their new power and glory, and became the XXVth Dynasty amongst the Pharaohs of Egypt. We can see their names carved in Egyptian temples, and know that they felt that they now took their place in the long line of Egyptian rulers. They surrounded themselves with all the pomp and adoration due to a Pharaoh, and wore the double crown, the crown of Upper and Lower Egypt. However, they were not able to restore Egypt to her former position of power in the ancient world, and she is referred to as a 'bruised reed, on which if a man lean, it will go into his hand, and pierce him; so is Pharaoh king of Egypt unto all that trust on him'. The Pharaoh to whom this refers was Taharqa, the son of Piankhy. Taharqa came to the throne in 683 B.C. and in that year there was the most tremendous Nile flood which was regarded as a good omen for his reign, and which he described in an inscription found at Kawa, in Sudanese Nubia. This is what he says:

> It (the flood) penetrated the hills of Upper Egypt, it overtopped the mounds of lower Egypt, and the land became a primordial ocean . . . moreover the sky rained in Nubia, it made all the hills glisten. Every man had abundance of everything,

24

Egypt was in happy festival . . . For the inundation came as a cattle thief, it inundated the entire land, the like of it was not found in writing in the time of the ancestors and none said 'I have heard from my father (of such).'

Taharqa lived at Tanis, in the Egyptian Delta, so that he could keep a close watch on affairs in Asia Minor. In the course of time, in 671 B.C., Egypt was attacked by the Assyrians, and they drove Taharqa back as far south as Memphis. Taharqa was strong enough to counter this blow, and in 669 B.C., he temporarily drove the Assyrians out again; but in spite of the good omen of the flood, he could not hold Egypt against the enemy and he was driven out. He died in 663 B.C. and was succeeded by his nephew Tanwetamani. It was during the reign of Tanwetamani that the Assyrians drove the Kushites finally out of Egypt. Tanwetamani had pushed his way back as far north as Memphis, but on hearing of the arrival of the Assyrians once again, he sought refuge in Thebes, and their nearer approach sent him in flight to Napata, his capital in his own homeland. Thebes was sacked most brutally by the Assyrians, and the prophet Nahum, in warning Nineveh, an important town in western Asia, of the fate that awaited her, quoted the sack of Thebes. 'Art thou better than Ne-amen (Thebes)?' he asked, 'that was situate among the canals and had the Nile around it for a rampart and a wall? Kush and Egypt were her strength . . . Yet was she carried away, and she went into captivity; her young children were dashed in pieces at the top of all the streets; and they cast lots for her honourable men, and all her great men were bound in chains.'

The Kushites returned to Napata and ruled in their own country from this time onward. This did not prevent them, however, from styling themselves Kings of Upper and Lower Egypt, though they never again held power there. They did manage to penetrate north as far as Kalabsha, in Egyptian Nubia, and from time to time controlled the Nile as far north as this town. How far south their kingdom extended we do not know, but probably at least as far as Sennar and Kosti where objects with the names of Kushite kings have been found.

Until sometime during the sixth century B.C., Kush was ruled from Napata. Her kings and queens were buried in cemeteries nearby, and her great religious centre continued to flourish

The word 'Meroë' written in Egyptian and Meroitic hieroglyphs and in Coptic and Greek writing, as found in ancient texts.

The excavation of Meroë. (*University of Liverpool.*)

at Jebel Barkal across the river. There had always been a branch of the royal family living at Meroë, however, as we know from the people who are buried there, and it seems probable that Meroë had always been an important provincial town within the kingdom. Sometime during the sixth century, possibly about 540 B.C., the royal family moved from Napata to Meroë which then became the capital city. The reasons for this move are not known, but we can guess at them.

The ruins of the city of Meroë lie about one hundred and twenty miles north of the capital of the modern Sudan, Khartoum, and close to the river. The land to the north of Meroë is semi-desert land, a sandy waste sparsely covered with thorn bushes and salty desert grass at most times of the year, rather barren except for the strip of river bank which is made fertile by the Nile's waters. At the time of the flood, in July or August each year, the Nile rises, and beyond soaking the dry earth, it brings with it a mass of rich silt which is deposited in layers on the river banks. But Meroë lies at the northern edge of the belt of annual rainfall, and so has the benefit of rain as well as of the river's floods, and this means that a much greater expanse of land is cultivable – wherever the rain falls, crops can be grown, on the plains and in the water courses. This part of the Sudan is often called the 'Island of Meroë'. You will see from the map that it is not strictly an island at all, but its good fortune in having the floods of two rivers, the Nile and its tributary, the Atbara, and annual rain, make it appear an island of fertility as one travels down from

26

the north. Nowadays it is not much cultivated except along the river banks, but at the time of the rain the whole area is covered with grass, in the places where no crops have been sown, and is used by nomad tribesmen as pasture for their herds. This is a matter of some importance, for without the possibility of cultivation of crops and herds on a scale larger than that permitted by river bank cultivation, the kingdom of Kush would have been unlikely to attain the power and importance which in its time it enjoyed.

This may well be the reason why the Kushite kings moved their capital south. They were wealthy and probably had huge herds to feed which would increase in the better pasture lands, and in fact it must have been difficult to find much cultivable land round Napata. In addition to this, Meroë stood on the river bank near to a crossing point for the caravans which carried trade east and west – their route followed the River Atbara into the Abyssinian hills and thence to the Indian Ocean. A third reason was that Meroë had become a centre of iron working, a metal of increasing use at that time, and this would have made it a place of importance.

Of the period when Kush was in close contact with Egypt, either as subject state or ruler, we are able to read of events which were recorded by the Egyptians in hieroglyphs. There are also records, inscriptions in hieroglyphs again, which the Kushites made themselves, as for example Taharqa's inscription at Kawa about the flood. Later on, although the Kushites continued for a time to use

An offering table showing 'Meroitic cursive' script.

Map showing the 'Island of Meroë' and the antiquities found there.

27

Bound captives, engraved on a bronze bowl.

hieroglyphs, they altered them slightly and began to use them for a language of their own, so that while the words can be read and pronounced, we do not know what they mean, except for a few titles of royalties and officials, and proper names. Later still, they developed their own writing, known to the scholars who are trying to translate it as 'Meroitic cursive' writing, and here again, although the words can be read, we have as yet no idea what they mean. And so, it is only when people of other tongues, whose languages are known to us, came into contact with Kush that we can find out anything of the later historical happenings. This unfortunately was not often, or at least not enough was recorded, for us to have any clear idea of what was happening in Kush, particularly after the capital was removed to Meroë. By this time, it had clearly become a wealthy and important kingdom, as we can tell from the remains of Meroë, and the objects which have been found there; and from the pictures carved on the walls of the temples, it would seem that there must have been many battles, for the kings and queens of Kush are seen trampling on their enemies and viewing long lines of bound captives. But who their enemies were, and where their battles, we cannot say.

Both Kush and Meroë itself were well known in the ancient world. In the Bible, in the Acts of the Apostles, we can read of an Ethiopian (as the Kushites were often called at this time) who went to Jerusalem, 'a man of great authority under Candace, queen of the Ethiopians, who had charge of all her treasure', and who was converted to Christianity. The Meroitic word for queen (Candace) is used, though it was misunderstood by the writer as being the name of a particular queen when in fact it is a general word as is our 'queen'.

A Roman writer, Strabo, gives us an account of a historical event which was of great significance for Meroë. This was at a time when the Romans were ruling Egypt and had established their frontier at Syene (Aswan). The Roman Governor of this part of Egypt, a man called Gaius Petronius, who held this office from 25 to 21 B.C., left his frontier post with many of his troops to cam-

Egyptian wall painting of Nubians paying tribute.

paign in Arabia. Taking advantage of his absence, the Kushites attacked Syene and sacked it, carrying off the statue of the Emperor Augustus which the Romans had set up in the market place. On his return, Gaius Petronius was extremely angry at the news which greeted him, and determined to punish the Kushites for their daring, so at the earliest opportunity, probably about 23 B.C., he set out on a reprisal raid against them. Strabo tells us that the poorly armed Kushites could not compete with the Romans and were driven back further and further until Gaius Petronius finally reached Napata, the ancient capital of Kush (by now the capital was well established at Meroë) and sacked it. At last the Kushites were forced to give in, and sent ambassadors to Samos to see the Roman Emperor and sue for peace. We are told that the commander of the Kushite forces was a general of Queen Candace (Strabo makes the same mistake as the writer of the biblical reference in thinking that Candace was her name) and from evidence found in excavating the tombs at Meroë, it seems likely that Queen Amanirenas was the queen concerned. It is interesting that there are two inscriptions on stone tablets which mention this queen, both in Meroitic, so that they cannot be understood; both link her name with that of a Prince Akinadad, and it may be that these inscriptions give an account of the same events from a Meroitic point of view. But the most interesting point about this story is that in the course of excavations that were carried out at Meroë, the head of a statue was found hidden in a pocket of sand under the threshold of a doorway in one of the palaces. It was clearly the head of Augustus and was of Roman workmanship. It can be seen now in the British Museum, and it is tempting to think that this is the head of the statue which the Kushites stole from Syene market place and hid carefully away, for fear the Roman soldiers should find it.

The head of Augustus, which was found at Meroë. (*British Museum.*)

There were other Roman expeditions to Kush, but it is by no means certain that they were military expeditions, even though soldiers took part in them. In a Greek papyrus dated about

29

An Axumite inscription written in
Greek and found at Meroë.

A.D. 64, we read of a skirmish in the desert between the Romans
and the 'Ethiopians' (Kushites) and we know that some soldiers
of the Emperor Nero went through Kush and far south of Meroë
towards the heart of Africa. Seneca, another Roman writer, tells
us of their exploits, and it seems that they came to huge marshes,
which must be the *sudd* of the southern Sudan 'where the river is
so entangled that only small boats carrying one man can pass'.
These soldiers did not think Kush worth a second visit, finding it
a harsh and inhospitable land, and their journey was certainly
more for exploration than with any military intent.

So we learn little of any historical events of this time, beyond
the sacking of Napata by Petronius's troops, and there is ample
evidence of this in broken statues at Jebel Barkal and signs of fire
amongst the ruins. From excavation of the burial places at Meroë,
we can see that the graves became poorer and less well built, and
the grave goods fewer and less valuable; on occasion things were
even taken from earlier graves, and the name of the newly dead
person was scratched – badly, for writing also deteriorated – over
the name of the earlier one. It seems that Meroë grew gradually
poorer, and probably did not continue to keep up contact with the
more prosperous countries to the north, and there must have been
much weakening tribal warfare with near neighbours.

The most powerful of Kush's neighbours were the Axumites,
people from the southern tip of Arabia who had settled across the
sea from their homeland and made a kingdom on the western coast
of the Red Sea – the kingdom of Axum. As the power and wealth
of Meroë waned, the Axumite kingdom was becoming more and
more important and probably annexed much of Meroë's trade.
From an inscription of their King Aezanes, we learn that he sent
an army to crush Kush, probably using some border skirmishing
as an excuse for dealing this blow. We do not know exactly when
this was, but probably about A.D. 350. This is what Aezanes
says: 'Twice or thrice they had broken their solemn oaths, and
had killed their neighbours without mercy, and they had stripped
our deputies and messengers whom I sent to enquire into their
raids, and had stolen their weapons and belongings. And as I had
warned them, and they would not listen but refused to cease from
their evil deeds and betook themselves to flight, I made war on
them ... They fled without making a stand, and I pursued them
for twenty-three days, killing some and capturing others ... I

30

burnt their towns . . . and my armies carried off their food and copper and iron . . . and destroyed the statues in their temples, their granaries, and cotton trees and cast them into the River Seda (Nile)'. So Kush was conquered and falls into silence as complete as if it had never been. What happened to the people who fled without making a stand? Some scholars have suggested that they fled westwards and possibly settled in the area round Lake Chad, but as yet we have no positive evidence that this is what happened and await proof in the shape of some traces of their culture outside the kingdom of Kush.

Animals engraved on a bronze mirror.

This is all that is known or can reasonably be surmised about the history of Kush at present. What do we know of the Kushites themselves, and of the way in which they lived? Not very much unfortunately, but some of their towns, temples, and burial places have been excavated and studied by archaeologists. Apart from the buildings themselves and the pictures often carved or painted on them, objects have been found which the Kushites used; jewellery, pottery, glass, metalware, tools and weapons, and various objects which were used as part of their ritual in burying the dead have been found, and all can tell us something about the people who made and used them.

First of all, we must notice that the Kushites were an African people. Their close links with Egypt made them assume an Egyptian style in many things perhaps, but if we look at the statues, wall carvings, and paintings of Kushites it is clear that it is Africans who are represented. In their wall paintings, the Egyptians showed the Kushites as having dark skins in contrast to their own lighter ones, and sometimes drew their hair differently. The Kushites' own wall carvings on their temples showed their queens as plump rounded ladies, and quite different from the very slender ladies portrayed by the Egyptians. The great statues of the kings found at Jebel Barkal, although entirely Egyptian in style, show African features. A vase found in a grave at Faras, where there was an important Kushite settlement, shows how a Kushite artist saw his countrymen. Their language is thought to be an African language and scholars are trying to find a modern African tongue which might be the key to the understanding of Meroitic, as the Kushite language is usually called. The Kushites were the first truly African people to achieve a position of power and importance and to win the respect of the civilized world as it was at that time.

A painted vase showing a Kushite attacked by a lion.

31

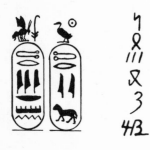

The name Tanyidamani written in Egyptian hieroglyphs, Meroitic 'cursive' script, and, below, in Meroitic hieroglyphs.

To learn something of the way in which the Kushites lived, we can look at the city of Meroë, which was partially excavated some years ago. The ruins extend over a wide area and it must have been a town of some size. It lies close to the River Nile, and the ruins of a stone built quay were discovered there where barges plying their trade along the river would have tied up. To the east of the town rises a ridge of low sandstone hills encircling the plain, and on its slopes, a row of pyramids of one of the Kushite cemeteries can be seen standing out sharply against the blown sand. Only a small part of Meroë has been excavated but here were found temples, two palaces, an elaborate, if rather rough, copy of a Roman swimming bath, and some ordinary dwelling houses. The remainder of the town is a jumble of mounds covered with broken red brick, and great piles of iron slag, the debris from Meroë's famous iron working. What lies under the mounds has yet to be discovered.

The ordinary houses were all built in the same style, a very common one in Africa, and which can be seen today in many places, including the northern part of the Republic of the Sudan, the home of Kush. This style consists of an open courtyard surrounded by a series of rooms, arranged to suit the owner, and it is convenient and adaptable – obviously the larger the courtyard, the greater the number of rooms which can be built around it. The rooms all open on to the courtyard, and entrance to the house is by a single door set in the outside wall. The two palaces were built in exactly the same style, but the plan of the rooms was more complicated than in the simpler houses, and one of them had a big verandah. On a bronze bowl that was found at another Kushite settlement, Karanog, now in Egyptian Nubia, there is an engraved design of a country scene showing reed huts in which the country people and perhaps the poorer townsmen may have lived. These are neatly

32

made, in the engraving at least, and are like elongated beehives with an arched doorway, and the reeds are gathered together at the top and tied to prevent them from falling apart. Right on top of the hut, a round pot seems to be balanced.

Of the things which they used in their houses, grindstones, pottery, baskets and simple tools of stone, such as arrowheads for hunting, or metal knives, axeheads, swords and razors have all been found. In the houses of the wealthy some of the fine imported wares would probably have been found – glass bottles, bowls and lamps of bronze or silver, exotic jewellery, most of which reached Kush through Egypt, or through Red Sea ports such as Adulis.

Meroitic pottery survives in great variety. The ordinary 'kitchen' ware, the cooking pots, beer pots, and bowls and basins for home use were heavy and often hand-made, probably by the women of the house, as is still the custom for certain types of container in the land that used to be Kush. The shapes are ordinary useful ones, bowls with or without an out-turned rim, some having lips for pouring liquids. The beer pots are like enormous flasks and are so common that it is clear that the Kushites much enjoyed their beer. Many of these types of pot are still in use with much the same kind of decoration and finish, and they are typically African pots meant for ordinary use. The finer pottery was of a high standard, wheelmade, of a fine hard paste, and decorated with a variety of designs. The most essentially Kushite of these decorations were those which were painted on to the pot with colours made by grinding different coloured earths, ('ochres' as they are called) the colours varying from yellow to red or brown. The designs themselves are unusually attractive, often consisting of a lively sketch of a person doing something, hunting perhaps, or of an animal, or of plants or flowers. Another type of decoration was the outlining of a design with little lumps of clay stuck on to the

33

A black pot with an impressed design in white, typical of Kushite workmanship. (*Ashmolean Museum.*)

A small vase showing 'barbotine' decoration.

A painted vase showing a hunter and his dog.

outside of the pot, the lumps sometimes being painted a different colour from the rest of the pot. The effect is of a raised design, and this is called 'barbotine' ware. It was very well known in the Roman world, and there is the possibility that pottery with this kind of decoration was imported rather than made locally. Other designs were made by scratching or punching the surface of the pot with a pointed stick, or a fish's spine, or a piece of bone before the clay was dry. All the pots are delightful both in shape and decoration, and the Kushite potters attained a very high standard and an individual style – each of the painted pots is a separate creation, the like of which has not been found elsewhere, and the scratched or punched designs are common all over Africa.

The wealthier of the citizens of Meroë may well have used the glass bottles and vases, and the bowls, lamps and other vessels made of copper, bronze or silver which were imported from Egypt at the time of the Ptolemies, and of the Romans. The Ptolemies were Greek, and came to power after Alexander the Great seized Egypt in 332 B.C., the first Ptolemy being one of his generals; and in time they were pushed out by the Romans – Julius Caesar turned Egypt into a Roman province in 30 B.C. Both the Greeks and the Romans brought their own ideas of art and culture to Egypt, and no doubt the people of Meroë who came into contact with these new ideas found them attractive. One of the Meroitic kings, Ergamenes, who ruled from about 248–220 B.C., was said to have had a Greek tutor, and he was certainly friendly enough with Ptolemy IV to join him in the building of two temples – one at Philae where Ptolemy built the inner hall, and Ergamenes the entrance hall, and a second at Dakka where this arrangement was reversed. It was at this time when relations between Kush and Egypt seem to have been particularly friendly that most of these foreign wares were brought into Kush, and it must have been a time when trade was very good. These vessels which were imported were rather elaborate and were probably not the best examples of the metalworkers' art at this time – they are interesting and important more because they indicate the wealth and position of Meroë as a centre of trade than for their own beauty. All these things have been found as grave goods, things which were buried with the dead for their use in the next world, and they do not occur in the latest graves when the greatness of Meroë was diminishing and trade and contacts with the outside world grew less.

The Kushites were themselves workers in metal, taught originally no doubt by Egyptian craftsmen, for in the early days of the kingdom the things which were made were exactly like Egyptian ones. They worked in bronze, copper, silver, and gold, and amongst other things made some heavy gold jewellery which the later queens wore, and which was buried with them. Necklaces, rings, earrings, and bracelets have all been found amongst the grave goods of the later queens, and like the painted pottery, they are strongly Meroitic and could not be confused with the work of any other place. This is at least partly because the workmanship shows all the craft of the Mediterranean world, but the designs have the character of Africa. One of the most interesting features of this culture is that the Kushites took and used what they found attractive or useful from the civilizations with which they came into contact, yet their own character was never submerged. Meroë lay at the end of a formidable journey, up river, through cataracts, and across desert, and it is surprising that she managed to keep so closely in touch with the fashions which really belonged to the Mediterranean world. Two other countries seem to have made some impression on Kush, Arabia, on the other coast of the Red Sea, and India. Arabia was more of a desert land than Kush, and had to find some way of storing water. The Arabians learned to build tanks and reservoirs, often hollowed out of the rock, to store their water, and the numerous reservoirs which belonged to the Kushites are thought to have been copied from Arabian examples, though there is no direct evidence that this was so. Indian influence is seen perhaps in the three-headed lion god, Apedemak, who sometimes had two sets of arms, an idea which was common enough in India, but unheard of in Egypt whence the Kushites took most of their gods. A picture of a Meroitic king riding an elephant, which is unique in this part of Africa, was possibly also inspired by India, for African elephants are known to be difficult to train for domestic purposes, whereas Indian elephants are adaptable, and are often used for riding. The wealth of Kush was based on trade, for she could produce things which were traditionally African trade goods, some perhaps from beyond her own borders, things which were much sought after in Egypt, and no doubt further afield. Gold, ivory, ebony, slaves, gum, animal skins and ostrich feathers all came from Kush, and the people prospered.

Religion played an important part in the lives of the Kushites as

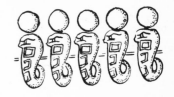

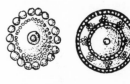

Examples of gold jewellery: bracelet, ear studs, two amulets, one of a cowrie shell, the other of a fly.

A king riding an elephant.

The lion god Apedemak.

is shown by the number of fine temples which still stand, though in ruins. As has been mentioned earlier, the religious centre was at Jebel Barkal, the holy hill which lay across the river from Napata. Before Kush became an independent kingdom, Jebel Barkal had long been a place of religious importance and the centre for what was then the southernmost part of the Egyptian empire. It was well established by the time Kush became independent, and there were several temples there, of which the largest, the temple of Amun, was second in size only to the great temple at Karnak in Egypt, dedicated also to Amun. This is an indication of the importance of Jebel Barkal. Here lived a colony of Egyptian priests who carried out religious rites and practices as they had learned them in Egypt, and no doubt they provided priests to take charge of all the temples in Kush. Later perhaps they may have trained Kushites in the priesthood.

For a long time Kushite religion seems to have been practised exactly as in Egypt, as one would expect, but as the close contact with Egypt became less and the priests were less in touch with their colleagues, some differences became noticeable – as for example, the introduction of an entirely new god, the lion god, Apedemak. He is not seen in the northern part of the kingdom, however, and appears only in temples near Meroë, so that he must have been revered only by the later Kushites.

One of the things everybody knows about the ancient Egyptians is that some of their dead kings and queens were buried in pyramids, some of them so huge, that we marvel at the ability to build such monuments. Kushite kings and queens also had pyramids, but theirs were of a different shape and much smaller. They were much more sharply pointed, and even the largest was tiny compared with the majority of Egyptian ones. Otherwise they were similar – stone faced pyramids, with a little chapel built against the east wall, under which ran a flight of steps leading to the burial chamber. The burial chambers were cut into the rock underground and were sometimes plastered and painted with appropriate scenes, such as the dead king adoring the gods. The tomb of King Tanwetamani, which is well preserved, has a particularly beautiful ceiling – dark blue like the night sky, covered with golden stars. In some of the earlier tombs, the dead person was laid to rest on a bed, but later great stone coffins, called 'sarcophagi', were used, which exactly copied Egyptian ones. In

the tombs were placed all the things which had been most precious
to the dead person in life, and which would be useful to him in the
after life, along with food, drink, and a retinue of servants, in the
form of little figures of faience or stone called 'Shawabtis', who
would perform the tasks which were asked of him and lighten his
load. The walls of the chapels were carved with scenes of offerings
being made to the gods, or the souls of the dead being carried on
a boat to be judged before the throne of the god Osiris.

There were several cemeteries containing royal pyramids – at
El Kurru, Nuri, and Jebel Barkal in the northern part of the kingdom, and three near the town of Meroë. These of course contained
only the burials of the royal family. The ordinary people were
buried less elaborately, in simple graves in the earth, though these
were often brick lined and had a special bench cut into the side to
use as a resting place. Here too precious objects were placed to
accompany the dead – pots, jewellery, a hunter's favourite bow, a
child's toy.

With the strong influence of Egypt on their religion, it is not
surprising that the Kushites built their temples in the Egyptian
style. You will remember Taharqa, one of the earlier Kushite

A Shawabti made of faience from a
royal tomb. Faience is a material
made of powdered quartz which is
then glazed, usually in a blue or
green colour.

37

kings, who ruled Egypt as well as Kush. He left an inscription at Kawa telling of the way in which he rebuilt a somewhat ruined mudbrick temple, and made it into a fine one to honour the god and bring merit to his homeland – and, perhaps, himself as well! This is part of what he says in the inscription:

And His Majesty caused his army to go to Gem-Aten (the ancient name for Kawa) together with numerous gangs and good craftsmen innumerable, an architect being there with them to direct the work at this temple while His Majesty was in Memphis. Then this temple was built of good white sandstone, excellent, hard, made with enduring work, its face being towards the west, the house being of gold, the columns of gold, the inlays thereof being of silver. Its towers were built, its doors erected, it being inscribed with the great name of His Majesty. Its numerous trees were planted in the ground, and its lakes dug, together with its House of Natron, it being filled with implements of silver, gold, bronze, whereof the number is not known. And this god was made to rest within it, resplendent, glorious for ever, the reward for this being life, welfare, and the appearance upon the throne of Horus for ever. Trees and vines were planted – all abundant timber, innumerable – cedar, juniper, acacia. His whole city was made to glisten with trees of all kinds . . . Wine is trodden from the vines of this city.

And to lend final glory to the temple, Taharqa sent the wives of the Egyptian princes whom he had conquered to be handmaidens to the god.

Other temples have been found and studied, mostly in the Island of Meroë and in Meroë itself. Some of these are in Egyptian style, but a few later ones have an air of Greek or Roman architecture about them. At Meroë, the most impressive building was probably the temple of Amun, the great god of Egypt, built in the Egyptian style, and now only a crumbling sandstone ruin. In its time, it must have been a grand building, with sandstone columns and pyloned doorways, much of it carved with scenes of gods receiving homage and gifts, and portraits of the kings and queens who had built or altered the temple. Some of the temple rooms were painted with colours, the reds, blues, yellows, and browns known to us from Egyptian temples, all brilliant against a sparkling white background. These colours were used either for a formal

The head of a statue of King Nete-kamani.

decoration, such as a pattern of leaves round a column, or for more elaborate scenes. Leading up to this temple was a long avenue of stone rams, with gentle faces and curled fleeces, of which a few still remain in position.

Another temple, the 'Sun Temple', was discovered on the edge of Meroë. It was well known in the ancient world, and was described by Herodotus, the Greek historian and traveller whom we have mentioned before. He says: 'This Table of the Sun is said to be a meadow, situated in the outskirts of the city, where a plentiful supply of boiled meat of all kinds is kept; it is the duty of the magistrate to put the meat there at night, and during the day anybody who wishes may come and eat of it. Local legend has it that the meat appears spontaneously, and is the gift of the earth'. The ruins of the temple stand in a hollow which collects more rain-water than the flatter land around it, so grass grows better there, and it is in fact a kind of meadow. The temple itself was not very big, and was built on a platform raising it above the level of the ground, and consisted of a cloister of columns surrounding the inner holy place, the sanctuary. This temple must have been most attractive, for the floor and walls of the sanctuary were covered with blue and yellow tiles, those of the walls being the blue of the

39

The 'kiosk' at Naqa. (*University of Chicago.*)

sky. When one looked at it against the sky, it must have appeared quite insubstantial and ethereal. A great golden disc to represent the Sun was built into the wall facing the entrance, honouring the God to whom the temple was dedicated. On the outer wall of the platform, scenes were carved into the stone to show the defeat and slaughter of the enemies of Kush, and the triumphal procession of the Kushites. This temple is built in a style which copies Greek ideas of architecture, though the carvings and the sun disc are purely Meroitic.

Some miles away from Meroë, in what is now a stretch of sandy scrubland but which is the site of another Meroitic town, lies a group of four more temples. Three of these are Egyptian in style, and have some fine wall carvings for decoration, including the best preserved representation of the lion god, Apedemak. The fourth temple is a mixture of Egyptian and Roman styles. This is at a place called Naqa, and the little temple is known as the 'kiosk'.

40

From a distance it looks like a Roman building, but closer inspection shows that much of the decoration is Meroitic. Nevertheless, it is a remarkable building to find so far south in the African continent, where the Romans themselves never lived, and hardly even visited.

It is only from studying the buildings, the temples, pyramids and other graves, and the objects which were found in them that we know anything about the Kushites in the later days of their kingdom. From these studies it becomes clear that it was a wealthy kingdom, able to import and use goods and ideas from further afield, mainly from Egypt. From the evidence which they have found, archaeologists believe that the greatest period of the Kushite kingdom was from about 250 B.C. until the beginning of the second century after the birth of Christ. It was at this time that the pyramids were filled with the finest objects, and when many great monuments were built. Trade was at its height, and was far flung, and most important of all, the working of iron had become well established.

For Meroë itself, and for the rest of Africa, this was perhaps the most important contribution of Kushite culture and achievement. Iron had been known and used in Asia Minor for many years, probably since about 1500 B.C., and in conquering Egypt, the Assyrians had the advantage of iron weapons over the Egyptians' bronze ones. Yet iron remained rare in Egypt, at least partly because they had little iron ore in their country. In Kush, there was iron ore, but no iron objects have been found amongst the grave goods in the pyramids until the burial of King Harsiotef who died sometime between 370 and 360 B.C. Earlier than this, in about 430 B.C., Herodotus tells us the Kushites bound their prisoners with gold chains, and used weapons tipped with stone, while for them, bronze was the rarest metal. It was only when the capital of Kush was well established at Meroë that iron started to be used extensively for here not only was the ore available in plenty, but there were trees to burn for charcoal to smelt it with. Iron was fashioned into tools and weapons on a large scale, judging by the huge piles of slag which are one of the most striking features of the ruins of the city of Meroë. Then, equipped with iron weapons to fight their enemies, and iron hoes to till the ground, the Kushites were far in advance of their neighbours. Although we have as yet no exact knowledge of the way in which it happened,

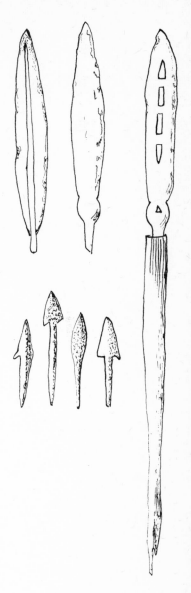

Examples of iron weapons found in the excavations at Meroë.

41

there is little doubt that understanding of the processes of iron smelting and the use of iron spread from Meroë through the rest of Africa, westwards to the people of the western Sudan, and southwards into the heart of the African continent.

There is much more to be found out about Kush, and further work in the ancient towns and temples and, above all, the eventual understanding of the language will increase our knowledge greatly. In other parts of Africa, we may find traces of their culture and discover what happened to the Kushites after they were defeated by the people of Axum, for it is hardly possible that a people who had achieved so much should disappear without leaving their mark somewhere.

A painted vase found in a grave, showing typical Kushite symbols: the snake, the lion and the lotus.

4. *Ghana, Mali, and Songhai*

Two of these names will be known to you as the names of modern African states, but the fact that they were also the names of powerful mediaeval states in West Africa is perhaps less well known. Yet at the time of their flowering, each one might have seemed well advanced in matters of government and economic prosperity, and certainly each played an important part in the development of West Africa. Each rose to power in its turn, and became a vital link in the commercial world of North Africa, which in its turn affected events in Europe – various European countries were dependent on their import of Ghana gold through North Africa for the stability of their currencies.

The modern boundaries of states in Africa have mainly been drawn by agreements between governments of European countries and fairly recently. Sometimes they appear to have been drawn with a ruler on a paper map sheet; at other times they follow the course of a river, or a line of hills, or some other natural boundary; but frequently they bear little relation to the people living on the ground, and tribes are sometimes separated over the borders between two countries, or may even have been subject to rulers of different nationalities. Fixed boundaries are comparatively new in Africa, and in days gone by people moved at will, restricted only by the kind of life they led; a forest dweller would not easily settle down in desert lands, nor a horseman in the forest; cattle owners travelled the grasslands, fishermen the rivers. So we must think of Ghana, Mali, and Songhai not as states with fixed boundaries settled by treaty or by force of arms, but as a people each of whom for a time became the most powerful group in a particular area. They used to exact tribute and levies – men to swell their armies in time of war, servants, supplies of grain, for example – from the people who were settled as cultivators round about; they were strong enough to enforce their demands. As their influence increased, and

43

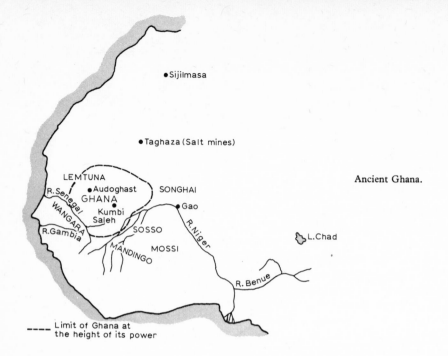

Ancient Ghana.

- - - - Limit of Ghana at
the height of its power

more land and people came under their control, the rulers would appoint 'provincial' officials to collect the tribute and keep an eye on things in general. The rulers claimed territory as their own but they were not rulers in the modern sense; they left the people to govern themselves in their own way, but expected obedience and a ready response to their demands.

GHANA

In this chapter, the Ghana of which we shall learn is the ancient state of that name. It has nothing to do with the modern state and was about 1000 miles north of it.

Ghana was the first of the three states to rise to power. Africans in those days did not write, but passed their stories, history sometimes, by word of mouth from generation to generation. Apart from this oral tradition, which has been mentioned before, what we know of the history of Ghana is based largely on the writings of Arab travellers, some of whom visited that country and some who merely reported what they had heard about it. It is likely that

44

Ghana had been a power in West Africa for some time, perhaps ever since the Romans left North Africa in the fourth century A.D. One writer, El Zuhri, tells us that the people of Ghana attacked neighbours "who knew not iron and fight with bars of ebony". The Ghanaians "defeat them because they fight with swords and lances".

We do not hear anything definite about Ghana until the eighth century, when an Arab writer, El-Fazari, tells us that the Arabs in Morocco sent an expedition to raid Ghana which he calls "the land of gold". This was about A.D. 734 and the Arabs were no doubt interested in capturing the source of the gold for which Ghana, even then, was famous. To the north of the land controlled by Ghana, and just south of the Atlas mountains, lay a town called Sijilmasa which was the meeting point for Arab and African traders. Here the Soninke of Ghana sent their gold to exchange for goods they wanted, and particularly for salt, of which there were no supplies further south. This was then taken south, and exchanged for gold, for the Soninke were not themselves gold miners; they simply acted as 'middlemen' or agents between the gold producers and the Arabs who wanted to acquire it. The Arabs in their turn sold or traded it into Europe. African markets were the main source of gold before the discovery of America, at least for Europe, and European states depended on 'Guinea gold' for their financial enterprises.

Gold was mined by a negro people in a district called Wangara, which lay outside the political control of Ghana, and to the south-west of it. It was these people who had a great appetite for salt and no supply of it in their own country. Copper, cloth, dried fruit, and cowrie shells were also traded and accepted in exchange for gold, but it was salt that the miners really wanted – so much so that it was said that they gave gold in equal weight to the salt they received. This trade in gold was described by Masudi, an Arab traveller again, writing a little before A.D. 950. He says: 'The kingdom of Ghana is one of great importance and it adjoins the land of the gold mines. Great peoples of the Sudan live there . . . They have traced a boundary which no one who sets out to them ever crosses. When the merchants reach this boundary, they place their wares and cloth on the ground and then depart, and so the people of the Sudan come bearing gold which they leave beside the merchandise and then depart. The owners of the merchandise then

A modern Ghanaian looks at a house in Kumbi Saleh.

return, and if they are satisfied with what they have found, they take it. If not, they go away again, and the people of the Sudan return and add to the price until the bargain is concluded.' ('Sudan' here refers to the Western Sudan – the Arabs called all the land south of the Sahara and north of the forest from west to east coasts 'Bilad es Sudan', which means the 'land of the blacks'). This is often called 'the silent trade' and is known from other writers, including Herodotus, as being a method of exchange used by people with no common language. There is a story that the greedy merchants, being anxious to discover the source of the gold, and perhaps mine it for themselves, cheated on one occasion and meanly captured one of the frightened Wangara, in the hope that he would show them where the gold was found. But he pined away and died without speaking, and so angry were the miners at this treachery that it was three years before they would trade their gold again, and then only because they needed salt so badly.

The value of the gold trade is not known, but apart from the profit on this, the Soninke rulers of Ghana found other ways of making money or of ensuring that their wealth should not decrease. They were clever enough to realize that they must control the *supply* of gold if they were to keep its 'price' up; if they let so much gold pass through their hands that it ceased to be much sought

46

after, it would become less valuable and they would get less in exchange. El Bekri, an Arab historian who tells us much about Ghana, says: 'All nuggets of gold that are found in the mines of this empire belong to the king; but he leaves to his people the gold dust that everyone knows. Without this precaution gold would become so plentiful that it would practically lose its value'. One nugget which the king owned was so large that it became famous, and all sorts of rumours were spread about its weight, varying from 30 lbs. to one ton! The king was said to tether his horse to it, so it must have been heavy.

In addition to regulating the supply of gold, Ghana also imposed taxes on every load of goods which entered or left the area over which it had political control. The gold trade was therefore highly organized, and it was on this that the wealth and importance of Ghana was based.

The most detailed description of Ghana at this time is given by El Bekri, who finished writing his book in A.D. 1067. He did not actually visit Africa himself, and was living in Spain, but from his work it is obvious that he had good information, much of it probably from travelled merchants and officials of various kinds. 'The king of Ghana,' El Bekri tells us, 'can put two hundred thousand warriors in the field, more than forty thousand of them being armed with bow and arrow.' This is a formidable army, and those who were not armed with bows and arrows would certainly have had iron weapons, swords and daggers, for hand-to-hand fighting.

The capital city of Ghana was really two separate towns lying about six miles apart. One of these was called 'El Ghaba', meaning 'the forest', and here the king lived and held his court. The king's residence consisted of 'a fortress and several huts with domed roofs, the whole being enclosed by a wall', while the ordinary citizens lived in huts made of acacia wood. This is what El Bekri tells us about the king's court: 'When he gives audience to his people, to listen to their complaints and set them to rights, he sits in a pavilion around which stand his horses dressed in cloth of gold; behind him stand ten pages holding shields and gold-mounted swords; and on his right hand are the sons of the princes of his empire, splendidly clad and with gold plaited into their hair. The governor of the city is seated on the ground in front of the king, and all around him are his viziers in the same position. The gate of the chamber is guarded by dogs of an excellent breed, who

A gravestone inscribed in Arabic from Kumbi Saleh.

47

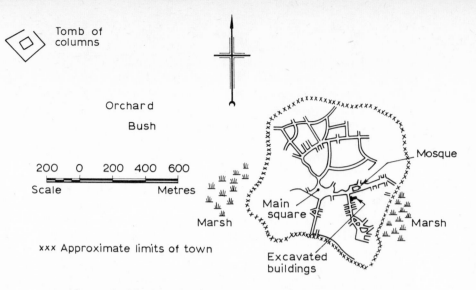

Tomb of columns

Orchard

Bush

200 0 200 400 600
Scale   Metres

xxx Approximate limits of town

Mosque

Main square

Marsh

Marsh

Excavated buildings

Plan of Kumbi Saleh. (*After Thom-assey & Mauny.*)

never leave the king's seat; they wear collars of gold and silver . . . The beginning of an audience is announced by the beating of a kind of drum which they call *deba*, made of a long piece of hollowed wood . . .' As they knelt before him, the king's own countrymen poured dust over their heads as a mark of respect, while the Muslims, traders and others clapped their hands to honour him.

The other city was built partly of stone houses and partly of straw-thatched mud houses. Here the Muslim population lived, the merchants, lawyers, religious teachers and others who had come to trade or live in Ghana. The site of this second city is known and a little excavating has been done there. It is at Kumbi Saleh, some 1000 miles north of modern Ghana, and on the southern border of what is now Mauretania. Mosques and houses have been uncovered from the desert sand, built of blocks of stone cemented together with mud. Some of the houses were very grand, two storeys high, with many rooms, and one of them showed the remains of the yellow plaster which had decorated the inside walls of the rooms. It was a big town covering a square mile, and from the style and size of the buildings and the things so far found in them, it gives an impression of great prosperity. More interesting perhaps is the mixture of Arab and African objects found – glass weights for weighing gold, pottery, verses from the Koran painted on stone tablets, and a fine pair of scissors, all of which must have come from the North by their style, together with farming tools and weapons of war which would have been made locally. So little

48

of Kumbi Saleh has been excavated that this is all we know about it as yet, and the site of El Ghaba has not yet been discovered.

We are told very little about the people of Ghana. They grew crops, (millet is mentioned), and they fished, and they were often required by their king to fight troublesome neighbours or to make raids for slaves, for trade in slaves was a secondary source of income to Ghana. El Bekri also gives us a description of a king's burial. He says: 'When the king dies, they build over the place where his tomb will be an enormous dome of wood. They bring him in on a bed . . . and put him inside the dome. At his side they place his ornaments, his weapons and the vessels from which he used to eat and drink. They also place there the man who had served his meals. They close the door of the dome and cover it with mats and materials and then they assemble the people, who heap earth upon it until it becomes like a large mound.' This was not an uncommon form of burial for royalty in ancient Africa, and shows us that the Soninke stuck to their own beliefs and traditions in spite of the powerful efforts of the Muslims to convert them to Islam.

Ghana was not able to develop and grow to power and prosperity in peace. There were continual quarrels and fighting between the Soninke and some of their stronger neighbours, the Lemtuna and

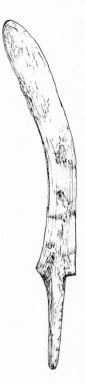

Iron sickle from Kumbi Saleh.

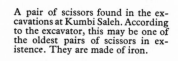

A pair of scissors found in the excavations at Kumbi Saleh. According to the excavator, this may be one of the oldest pairs of scissors in existence. They are made of iron.

Curved knife blade from Kumbi Saleh, made of iron.

49

the Jedala who lived to the north of Ghana. The Lemtuna captured from Ghana the town of Audoghast, which had been a tribute paying city, and a place of some importance. El Bekri tells us it was 'a very large city with several markets, many date palms and henna trees as large as olives . . . filled with fine houses and solid buildings'. Water was in plenty, and made possible the raising of a variety of crops; millet, dates, wheat, figs and vines are all mentioned. It was also involved in the caravan trade, and was an important trading centre like Sijilmasa, where gold and slaves were sent on their way north, and salt, cloth and dried fruit were despatched southwards. The Lemtuna living here were mainly 'white', that is to say they were Berbers, North African people like the Tuareg, and not negroes.

In North Africa there had grown up a sect of Muslims who wished to reform their faith, believing that people had become slipshod in their observance and were not strict enough in keeping to the word of the great prophet Mohammed. These people were called *el murabitin*, but are known nowadays as the Almoravids. They were fanatical, believing sincerely in the rightness of their own strict faith, and determined that everyone else should too. In A.D. 1042, the Almoravids set out on a holy war to convert the Muslims they considered slack and the pagans who had not known the benefit of their religion. Ultimately they reached the land of the Lemtuna, and captured Audoghast from them in A.D. 1054. The Lemtuna, being offered the choice of conversion to the faith of the Almoravids, or death, mostly chose conversion, and so joined their conquerors. Growing from strength to strength, largely by the power of their swords, the Almoravids attacked Ghana, but the Soninke were powerful enough to keep them at bay for some time, and their capital at Kumbi Saleh did not fall until A.D. 1076–7. But the Almoravids were not able to hold the land and peoples they had conquered, partly at least because they had split their forces and sent armies into Morocco and Spain. In A.D. 1087, their leader in the Sudan, Abu Bakr, was killed while quelling a revolt, and Ghana regained its independence.

However, the years under Almoravid rule had weakened Ghana's links with the people she had controlled, and her authority over them was lost in some of the former provinces. Some peoples split off and became separate kingdoms admitting no allegiance to Ghana, and her empire shrank, and never recovered. Writing in the fourteenth century, when the empire of Ghana had decayed, Ibn Khaldun, another Arab historian, tells us that the Almoravids 'spread their dominion over the negroes (here the Soninke), devastated their territory and plundered their property. Having submitted them to a poll tax, they imposed on them a tribute (that is the *payment* of tribute), and compelled a great many of them to become Muslims. The authority of the kings of Ghana being destroyed, their neighbours, the Sosso, took their country and reduced the inhabitants to slavery.' The date of this final downfall of Ghana was A.D. 1203, when Sumanguru, the greatest of the Sosso rulers, captured Ghana and enslaved the people. But Sumanguru overreached himself, and in A.D. 1235, while attempting to subdue the growing power of another people, the Mandingo, he was defeated and killed. Ghana became the territory of Sundiata, the Mandingo ruler, and part of the empire of Mali.

MALI

Like the ancient kingdom of Ghana, the Mali of which we shall learn here is also the ancient kingdom and not the modern state, though in the case of Mali the ancient and modern states cover more or less the same territory.

What the Mandingo were doing when Ghana was at the height of her power is not recorded, and we first hear of them in the middle of the eleventh century as rulers of a small state, Kangaba. They had been converted to Islam by the Almoravids, and were not then very powerful or important. In the thirteenth century they began to extend their kingdom and pushed towards the south and south-east. It was just at this time that the Sosso defeated Ghana, as we have seen, and they also were feeling their power and regarded the Mandingo as their rivals. At first, Sumanguru, the king of the Sosso, met with some success, and it is said that he arranged to have eleven brothers, who were the heirs to the throne of Mali, put to death so that he could take their place. A twelfth brother, Sundiata, was overlooked, perhaps because he was sickly and thought unlikely to live in any case, and this proved to be Sumanguru's undoing. For Sundiata thrived, and when he reached manhood the succession to the throne passed to him in A.D. 1230; he rallied his people, many of whom had been about to declare their allegiance to the Sosso, and in A.D. 1235 defeated and killed

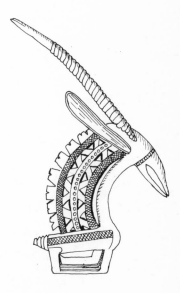

Wood carvings of the Bambara people who live in the area of ancient Mali.

● Sijilmasa

● Taghaza (Salt mines)

TUAREG

MALI

Walata ●

● Kumbi
Saleh

R. Senegal

WANGARA

BAMBUK

R. Gambia

Timbuktu ● Gao

● Jenné

● Kangaba
○ NIANI

MOSSI

SONGHAI

● Takedda
(Copper mines)

R. Niger

R. Benue

The kingdom of ancient Mali.

Sumanguru in a great battle. He then carried the war into the territory of the Sosso, and within five years managed to draw it into his own kingdom. This was the beginning of a great empire.

When the Sosso captured Ghana, the Muslim population moved out with all their possessions and settled in Walata, a town further north, and what remained of the city of Ghana was destroyed by Sundiata in A.D. 1240. In the same year, he moved his capital from Jeriba in Kangaba, the small state over which he had originally ruled, to Niani, a new city which he was building further down the Niger. Niani was usually called 'Mali', and it soon became one of the richest cities of the Sudan.

Sundiata decided that he must have a standing army, that is to say an army which was always ready to fight, consisting of men who were professional soldiers. He would then not have to rely on sending round his kingdom for men to build up an army every time he needed to fight a battle, as had been the custom in Ghana. In this way he was able to extend his territories, especially towards the west where he reached the river Gambia, enclosing the gold bearing districts of Wangara and Bambuk within his state, and equally important, he could control the lands and people under his rule. By the end of the thirteenth century Mali had become the richest and most powerful of the states of the Sudan, the gold trade was flourishing, and Sundiata, or Mari Jata as he was sometimes known, had become a hero to his people.

In A.D. 1307, the most famous of the Mandingo kings came to the throne. This was Mansa Musa, a grandson of Sundiata, and during his reign the name of Mali became known throughout the Mediterranean world and in Europe. This was largely because of Mansa Musa's fabled pilgrimage to Mecca, for the splendour of his caravan and the sensation which it caused made his name famous for years to come. He set out on this pilgrimage in A.D. 1324, surrounded by numerous followers and trains of camels loaded with gold and gifts, and passed through Walata and Tuat on his way to Cairo. He was mounted on a horse, no doubt with fine trappings, and 500 slaves went in front of him, each one bearing a staff of gold. He had supplied himself with large quantities of gold, and everywhere he went he made presents of it. So much of it came into circulation in Egypt that its value fell and had not recovered twelve years later when El-Omari, an Egyptian official who wrote about Mali, tells us of this famous visitor. Mansa Musa, as befits a good Muslim, was generous to the poor, and in the holy cities he visited, his gifts were especially large. His wealth and generosity and the simple, well-mannered behaviour of his followers made a good impression wherever he went, and the pomp and glory of his caravan was a matter for wonder and gossip for many years.

On his return journey, Mansa Musa heard that one of his generals had captured Gao, the capital of the Songhai, so he decided to visit this town and receive the submission of the Songhai king himself; and to make sure that the king did as he was told, he took the king's two sons back to Mali with him as hostages. The armies of Mali had not been idle while their king was making his pilgrimage, and by the time he returned to it, his kingdom stretched from the Atlantic in the west to the copper mines of Takedda in the east, from the fringes of the Sahara in the north to the gold bearing districts in the south.

Prosperity in trade brought with it wealth to Mali, and it also brought an increase in the culture and learning which for some time past had found a place in the Sudan. Wherever the Muslim population settled there was likely to be cultural activity, not necessarily by the merchants who probably formed the bulk of the Muslim population, but by lawyers, scholars and men of religion who settled with them. At this time Arab scholarship was second

These are designs which, it has been suggested, Mansa Musa brought from Cairo, and which now decorate houses in Walata.

53

A medieval map of Mali. The places referred to are Timbuktu, Mali and Gao. The writing says 'This Negro lord is called Musa Mali, lord of the Negroes of Guinea. So abundant is the gold which is found in his land that he is the richest and most noble king in all the land.'

to none, and Arab curiosity about the world in general and their neighbours in particular has, as we have seen, given us information of great value. At the time of which we are speaking, early in the fourteenth century, a body of scholars and men of letters, religious leaders, and others had settled at Timbuktu, which had become a cultural centre. When he was at Mecca, the most holy city of the Muslims and the destination of his pilgrimage, Mansa Musa had met a poet, a man from Andalusia in Spain called Es-Saheli, and persuaded him to enter his service. Es-Saheli was an architect as well as a poet, and when he reached Mali, he built some fine buildings. He is supposed to be the first man to have introduced burnt brick (the red brick which is now common) into the Sudan, and amongst the places he built were the great mosques at Gao and at Timbuktu (the Sankore mosque) and a palace for Mansa Musa to live in.

When he died in A.D. 1332, Mansa Musa left behind him a remarkable empire – wealthy, prosperous, well organized, and with cities renowned throughout the Sudan for their culture and learning. He

54

had also caused the fame of Mali to spread and put his empire literally on the map. Mediterranean and European map-makers began to show Mali on their maps, and even made some attempt to show would-be travellers how to get there. The king of Mali is described on one of these maps as 'This negro lord is called Musa Mali, Lord of the Negroes of Guinea. So abundant is the gold which is found in his country that he is the richest and most noble king in all the land.'

After Mansa Musa's death, the empire of Mali slowly grew weaker. He was succeeded by his son, Maghan, who was not the equal of his father. Maghan was unable to drive away the fierce Mossi, a people from the upper Volta, and lost Timbuktu to them, which city the Mossi burnt. Even worse for his empire was his trust in the two sons of the Songhai king, whom you will remember Mansa Musa had taken as hostages for the good behaviour of the Songhai people. They betrayed Maghan's trust, went back to Gao, and drove the Mandingo, the people of Mali, out of their kingdom, one of the brothers establishing himself firmly as king in his father's old capital. Gao was never recaptured by the Mandingo.

Sulayman, Mansa Musa's brother, who succeed his nephew Maghan, did what he could to rebuild the strength of the empire. During his reign, Ibn Battuta, a famous Arab writer and historian, visited Mali, and wrote an account of his visit. He was not very friendly at first, partly because he was kept waiting for a long time for an audience of the king, and was rather scornful of the people and their ways. A meal which was served to him of pounded millet mixed with milk and honey caused him to write that 'there was no good to be hoped for from these people'. He did not approve of the social position and freedom which the Mandingo women enjoyed, nor of the inheriting of property through the mother's side of the family, but since he was a Muslim, this is not surprising. 'A person's heirs are his sister's sons, not his own sons. This is a thing I have seen nowhere in the world except among the Indians of Malabar. But those are heathens: these people are Muslims, punctilious in observing the hour of prayer, studying books of law, and memorizing the Koran'. He sounds amazed and rather horrified, but for us it is interesting to notice that here again the influence of foreigners, however strong, did not cause an African people to give up their own ideas and practices. In the end, Ibn Battuta enjoyed his visit to Mali so much that he stayed for eight months.

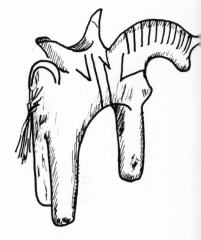

A child's toy, clay model of a horse.

He was much impressed with the *amount* of trade, and tells us that twelve thousand camels a year travelled one of the caravan routes alone, and caravans came from all directions. He found Mali so peaceful and settled that he was able to travel about with only two or three companions, and became convinced that he need not fear ill-will or rough treatment as had sometimes been his experience in other countries. 'They (the Mandingo) are seldom unjust, and have a greater dislike of injustice than any other people. Their sultan shows no mercy to anyone guilty of the least act of it. There is complete security in their country. Neither traveller nor inhabitant in it has anything to fear from robbers or men of violence.'

Ibn Battuta gives an impression of a peaceful and prosperous land, well organized in all ways – religion, justice, trade – and a happy people. However, the time of their greatness was passing, and little by little first one part of Mali was conquered and then another. The Tuareg captured Walata and Timbuktu, cities of trade and learning, and much of the northern part of the empire; the Mossi took parts of the south, and other peoples raided in the west. In the fifteenth and sixteenth centuries, the Mandingo appealed to the Portuguese, who by this time were settling on the coast of West Africa, for help in re-establishing their empire, but the Portuguese refused, for fear of upsetting other people with whom they hoped to do trade. So the great empire of Mali came to an end, and by the middle of the seventeenth century was back where it had started, in Kangaba, the original Mandingo state.

SONGHAI

The Songhai people lived on the banks of the middle Niger, as they still do, and in the seventh century, a Berber tribe, called the Dia, came down and imposed political control over them. The Songhai were farmers and fishermen, and the Dia ruled over them and gradually extended the area of land under their control. They also developed commerce and trading activities, as had the other big states of the Sudan, and exchanged goods with Ghana, Egypt and the countries of the North African coast. In the eleventh century they adopted the faith of Islam, probably because of influence from the Muslim countries with whom they traded, but the Songhai themselves were not much affected by Islam. At about the

ATLANTIC

OCEAN

----- Shows limit of
Songhai at the
height of its power

● Sijilmasa

● Taghaza

S O N G H A I

TUAREG

AIR

R.Senegal
Walata ●

Timbuktu ●
● GAO

● Agades

R.Gambia
Jenné ●
MOSSI

● Gobir
● Katsina

H A U S A

R.Niger
● Kano
● Zaria

L.Chad

R. Benue

The kingdom of the Songhai.

same time, a capital city was established at Gao, and judging by
Mansa Musa's delight at the capture of this city by his army, it
must have been a wealthy and important place. As we have seen,
Songhai became a tributary state of Mali for a time, from 1325
until 1335 when Ali Kohlen, one of the hostage brothers, restored
his people to independence. It was a perpetual struggle for the
Songhai to maintain their independence for they were pressed on
all sides, by Tuareg, by Mossi, by Mandingo, and others, all of
whom were anxious to extend their dominion.

About 1464, there came to the throne of the Songhai a king
called Sonni Ali. He was an able and ambitious man, if a little
ruthless, and hearing of some quarrelling and enmity amongst the
rulers of Timbuktu, he decided to take advantage of this and set out
with his army to capture that city. He entered Timbuktu in 1468,
and took it, killing many of the citizens. Then he decided to attack
Jenné, a town, like Timbuktu, celebrated for its trade and learning.
Jenné had had a rather more peaceful existence than Timbuktu as
it lay in a well watered, even marshy, area, and was more difficult
to attack. It took Sonni Ali some years to realize this ambition, but

57

A view of the town of Jenné. (*Prof. Ivor Wilks.*)

Jenné finally fell to him, probably about 1473. After this victory, he was much occupied with keeping the Mossi out of his kingdom, but by the time he died in 1492, he had established a fairly stable empire over much of the middle and upper reaches of the Niger. An Arab writer, Mahmud el Kati, describes him: 'He was always victorious. He directed himself against no country without destroying it. No army led by him in person was put to rout. Always conqueror, never conquered, he left no region, town or village . . . without throwing his cavalry against it, warring against its inhabitants and ravaging them.' In spite of his achievements, Sonni Ali had not been particularly liked by his people, for he was too cruel and too much of a dictator. When he died, the throne went to his son for only a few months, and was then usurped by one of Sonni Ali's generals with the support of the people. This general was a Muslim, called Mohammed Touré, and he took the title of Askia, being known as Askia Mohammed.

Sonni Ali had been a man of war and had forced allegiance to the Songhai kingdom over a wide area, and now Askia Mohammed set about organizing this kingdom into a properly administered state. He divided his kingdom into provinces and put a governor,

58

often a member of his own family or a trusted friend, in charge of each province. He created a number of central offices, almost like the Ministries of a modern government, to look after justice, finance, agriculture, and other matters of importance in the running of a state. He instituted a system of taxation whereby each town or district had its own tax collector, and he made some improvements which were designed to benefit trade, as for example putting an inspector in charge of each important market, and making weights and measures the same all over the kingdom. Apart from this kind of administrative reform, as a Muslim, he was sympathetic to the work of Muslims within his state, and encouraged them – the traders, and especially the learned men. Timbuktu, Jenné, and Walata flourished as centres of religion and learning; and as always when the Muslim population was settled and at peace trade flourished also and brought added wealth to Gao and Timbuktu. Sudan gold continued to flow northward, together with slaves, ivory, ebony and ostrich feathers, and in exchange came manufactured goods of copper and iron, brassware, sword blades from Spain and Germany, cloth, and of course salt. Timbuktu became a great centre, and its University, one of the first in Africa, was so famous that scholars came to it from all over the Muslim world.

Leo Africanus tells us much about the Western Sudan at this time. He was himself a most interesting person with a remarkable history. Born a Moor, he was captured by pirates when journeying on the Mediterranean sea as a young man; and the pirates, finding that he knew a great deal about African countries which seemed very remote to most people, gave him to Pope Leo XI in Rome as a present. The Pope was much impressed with his knowledge and set him free so that he could describe his travels and record what he knew. As a special favour he also gave him his own name – Leo.

He tells us of his journey to Walata, at that time the most northerly of the Songhai possessions, and of his pleasure at meeting such friendly people. "These people are black", he says, "but most friendly unto strangers." He visited Timbuktu, and after the fine Arab architecture of the North African states, he found the buildings rather poor and mean, "cottages built of chalk and covered with thatch", but evidently the buildings which Es-Saheli put up for Mansa Musa still stood, for Leo says: '. . . there is a most

The modern Sankoré mosque at Timbuktu. (*Prof. Ivor Wilks.*)

stately temple still to be seen, the walls whereof are made of stone and lime; and a princely palace also built by a most excellent workman from Granada.' He tells us something about the town: 'Here are many shops of artificers and merchants, and especially of such as weave linen and cotton cloth. And hither do the Barbary (North African) merchants bring the cloth of Europe. All the women of this region except maid-servants go with their faces covered, and sell all necessary victuals. The inhabitants, and especially strangers there residing, are exceeding rich, insomuch that the king that now is, married both his daughters to two rich merchants. Here are many wells containing most sweet water . . . Corn, cattle, milk and butter this region yields in great abundance: but salt is very scarce here, for it is brought hither by land from Taghaza which is five hundred miles distant."

At the time of Leo's visit, Askia Mohammed and his court happened to be at Timbuktu also and received Leo in audience. He must have been dazzled by the wealth and pageantry at the court and tells us:

The rich king of Timbuktu has many plates and sceptres of gold, some whereof weigh 1300 pounds; and he keeps a magnificent and well-furnished court. When he travels anywhere, he rides upon a camel which is led by some of his noblemen: and so he does likewise when he goes to warfare, and all his soldiers ride upon horses . . . They often have skirmishes with those that refuse to pay tribute, and, so many as they take, they sell unto the merchants of Timbuktu. Here are very few horses bred, and the merchants and courtiers keep certain little nags (horses) which they use to travel upon; but their best horses are brought out of Barbary . . .

Here are a great store of doctors, judges, priests and other learned men, that are bountifully maintained at the king's cost and charges. And hither are brought divers manuscripts of written books out of Barbary, which are sold for more money than any other merchandise. The coin of Timbuktu is of gold without any stamp or superscription: but in matters of small value they use certain shells (cowrie shells) brought hither out of the kingdom of Persia . . .

This was Timbuktu at the height of its prosperity, and other towns such as Jenné and Walata would have made a similar impression. After leaving Timbuktu, he travelled about the country and then came to Gao, Askia Mohammed's capital city. This was a great town, unwalled, where Leo tells us: 'The houses thereof are but mean, except those wherein the king and his courtiers remain. Here are exceeding rich merchants . . . It is a wonder to see what plenty of merchandise is daily brought hither, and how costly and sumptuous all things be. Horses bought in Europe for ten ducats, are sold again for forty and sometimes for fifty ducats a piece. There is not any cloth of Europe so coarse, which will not be sold here for four ducats an ell, and if it be anything fine they will give fifteen ducats for an ell . . . A sword here is valued at three or four crowns, and so likewise are spurs and bridles with other like commodities, and spices also are sold at a high rate: but of all other commodities salt is the most extremely dear.' It is clear that Askia Mohammed was ruler of a wealthy land, which had wide contacts for trading, and which was renowned for its distinguished scholars and centres of learning.

As soon as he assured himself of the prosperity and well-being of his kingdom, Askia Mohammed set out on a pilgrimage to Mecca, arriving in the holy city in 1497. There he gave 10,000 gold pieces as alms for the poor, and for the establishment and upkeep of a hostel for other pilgrims from the western Sudan. He also received official recognition of his position as king of the Songhai,

A boy using a muslim writing board.

a matter of some importance to him since, as you will remember, he was a usurper to the throne.

On his return from Mecca, he set about extending his kingdom, and subdued peoples to the west and the south, taking in all the land that had once belonged to Mali, and reaching almost to the shores of the Atlantic. Next he tackled the Hausa states to the east, which had previously been left in peace by the rulers of the great kingdoms of the Sudan.

The Hausa states extended eastwards from the Niger, towards Lake Chad, and the country was fertile and well watered. The people were farmers and traders, and their work in weaving, metal working, and leather was well known. Merchants had settled in their great walled towns, such as Gobir, Zaria, Kano and Katsina, and they were peace loving, putting up with Tuareg raids from time to time without much retaliation. They were not organized for war and fell an easy prey to Askia Mohammed. However, Askia Mohammed's victory here could not be complete unless he could also protect his new lands from the raiding Tuareg, so he was obliged to campaign against them too.

The Tuareg were aggressive and were largely nomadic, making raids on other peoples over a wide area. They were expert at living under the harshest conditions of desert life, and were extremely mobile on their fast camels, so that there was little point in trying to follow and attack them when they were raiding. They had some permanent settlements, in Air, and at Agades, and Askia Mohammed wisely attacked them there, and successfully overcame Tuareg resistance. He captured Agades, and took control of the trade routes through Air, important routes which led to Tunis, Tripoli and Egypt. All this had been accomplished by about 1515.

Askia Mohammed had created the largest and the wealthiest of all the kingdoms of the Sudan. It stretched from what are now the southern borders of Algeria, to the edge of the forest lands in the south; from almost the shores of the Atlantic in the west, to Agades and Air in the east. He had a well-administered state, probably the most highly organized of all the African states, with an efficient system of government; and with the support of the Muslim scholars, religious leaders and traders, he had made Songhai a great trading empire, and a centre of Muslim scholarship and learning.

Askia Mohammed, having become old and blind, was deposed in 1528 by his son, Musa. After him, there was a series of struggles for the throne and quarrelling in court circles, and no one of any note came to power, though Songhai continued to flourish.

The wealth and power of Songhai had been the envy of Morocco for some time. The Moroccans would certainly have liked to have under their own control the sources of the supply of gold out of which much of their own wealth was made. In 1589, El Mansur, the powerful and ambitious ruler of Morocco determined to attack the Songhai empire, a decision which shocked his counsellors and officials. They thought it impossible that an army could cross the Sahara desert with all the paraphernalia of war, the weapons, food, and transport animals, and arrive fit for fighting, to say nothing of inevitable battles with warlike Tuareg on the way. El Mansur replied that merchants had travelled the desert without any special aids and 'I, who am so much better equipped than they, can surely do the same with an army which inspires terror wherever it goes ... Today the Sudanese have only spears and swords, weapons which will be useless against modern arms. It will therefore be easy for us to wage a successful war against these people and to prevail over them.' El-Mansur not only convinced his officials of the possibility of success, he even inspired them with enthusiasm for the expedition. It was not as hopeless a venture as it may sound, for by this time the Moroccans had gunpowder and firearms, and once the real difficulty, the desert crossing, was dealt with, there was every expectation that the firearms would win over the Sudanese swords and spears.

63

El Mansur found a suitable commander for his desert army, a young Spaniard called Judar, and put 4000 soldiers under his command. This army consisted largely of Europeans, Christians captured in war (El Mansur had recently routed a Portuguese army in a big battle), or bought from the Barbary pirates, or European mercenaries, men willing to fight for any army so long as the pay was good; but there were Moroccan troops as well. Apart from his troops, Judar had something like 9000 transport animals to care for, and enough food and equipment for the men and animals. It was a most remarkable undertaking, and the approach of such a caravan could hardly be kept a secret from the people of Songhai. The journey alone took about six months, and during this time, travellers gave news of its progress to Askia Ishak, the Songhai king. He decided to make a stand at a place called Tondibi, thirty-five miles away from Gao, having for his army 18,000 cavalry and 9000 infantry. Judar's army had been so reduced by the perils of the desert crossing that he is said to have had only 1000 troops left to throw into the battle, but such was the advantage of gunpowder and firearms over the simple weapons of the Songhai that he won without difficulty, and in spite of very great bravery on the part of the Songhai. Those who survived the battle fled across the Niger to the south and never returned. 'From that moment everything changed', a historian of the time tells us, 'danger took the place of security; poverty of wealth. Peace gave way to distress, disasters, and violence . . .' Such was the sad but valiant end of the greatest empire of the Western Sudan.

The story of the rise of each of these peoples to a position of power is virtually the same in broad outline, and as one flowered and then died, another took over. Their trade with the countries of North Africa gave them a part in the activities of the world, and a vitally important part since it was they who provided the gold on which many countries depended for their finances.

Without losing in any way their own African character, these states became part of the Islamic world, Ghana less so than the other two perhaps, but even there the Muslims had their own city, you will remember, and the kings had Muslim advisers. This had two main advantages for the African states; firstly, that the strongly Muslim states of North Africa with which they did trade, Morocco, Algeria, Tunis, Egypt, were well disposed towards their brothers in religion and traded with them on a basis of friendship and

A Moroccan soldier at the time of Judar. (*Radio Times Hulton Picture Library.*)

mutual support. Had the Sudan states been strongly anti-Muslim, there might have been a very different story to tell. Secondly, Islam had the effect of unifying each state. The fact that the rulers of Ghana, Mali and Songhai demanded no more than allegiance and tribute of various kinds from the peoples who became subject to them, meant that control over them was really very loose, and if we take into account the size of the great states as well, we can see that without some common purpose, a subject king might well have stirred up revolt amongst his own people and his neighbours and the peaceful conditions under which power and prosperity grew would have been lost. While the ordinary people were perhaps not greatly affected by Islam, the rulers or their advisers were all Muslims and this created a bond probably much stronger than any rule of force and terror could have done.

West African trade routes. This map shows routes in use throughout the time when the ancient states of Ghana, Mali and Songhai were powerful, and also those of Kanem, Bornu, Ashanti and the Yoruba.

66

5. *Kanem–Bornu*

KANEM and Bornu are states of the Central Sudan, to the east and a little south of Ghana, Mali, and Songhai, but still well to the west of the Nile. Lake Chad, which lies within this area, has long been called one of the great cross roads in tropical Africa, and around its shores people from many different places met and mingled – it is even possible that the Kushites settled here when they fled from the Axumites. Its fertility was attractive to the desert nomads from the north, and having no natural boundaries, no desert, no mountains, no tropical forest, it was easy to move about in. Here there were settled communities of farmers and also nomadic herdsmen, driving their animals through the pasture lands, and they were subjected to frequent raids by the Berber and Arab tribes from the desert.

The early history of these people is full of myth and legend. The ancient So of Lake Chad 'appear in legend as giants of prodigious force, and surprising feats are celebrated in their name. With one hand they damned the rivers; their voices were so great that they could call from one town to another, and birds took flight in panic whenever one of them should cough . . . Even the earth bore their weight with difficulty.' These are the words of a modern French scholar, Lebeuf, who has done a lot of research round Lake Chad, and much of what we know about the So is due to his work. They built towns, and worked in metals, and made fine pottery, but we still do not know a great deal about them, not even where they came from, nor what sort of people they were. However, the fact that their name is preserved and their marvellous feats passed down the generations in legend makes it fairly safe to assume that they were one of the peoples who ultimately became part of the Bornu nation.

The Kanuri, the people of Kanem, and later of Bornu, claim to have come originally from the Yemen in Southern Arabia. This is one of their traditional stories, and while there is little evidence to support it, it seems likely that about A.D. 700 many different peoples moved from the region of the River Nile westwards towards Lake Chad. This was due to the invasion of North Africa by the Arabs, which had far-reaching effects in Africa, and was the cause of much movement of different peoples – several of the modern peoples of Nigeria, for example, also have traditional stories of a great trek from the east to their present homeland.

One of the peoples who moved towards Lake Chad was the Zaghawa, a dark-skinned nomad people from the desert regions. They were a little like the Tuareg. An Arab writer, el-Yaqubi tells us: 'The blacks who went westwards (formed) a number of kingdoms. The first is that of the Zaghawa who inhabit the place called Kanem. Their dwellings consist of huts of reeds. They have no use for towns.' They moved in and settled amongst the peoples they found already living there and perhaps because they were stronger and more forceful, or were better organized and able to impose their will on others, they seem to have provided the rulers – kings, whom in these early times they regarded as divine. El-Muhallabi writes, in about A.D. 985:

> They exalt and worship him (the king) instead of God. They imagine he does not eat for his food is introduced into his compound secretly, no one knowing whence it is brought. Should one of his subjects happen to meet the camel carrying

Boy sitting by a pot typical of the So people; their pots are unusually large.

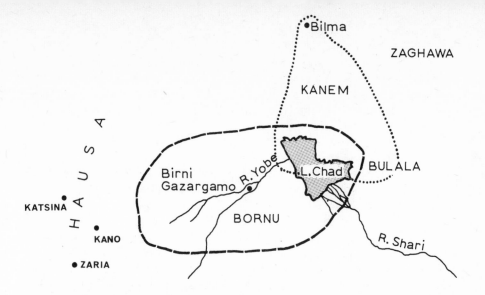

Map showing the extent of the early state of Kanem and the boundaries of the later state of Bornu overlapping it.

his provisions he is killed instantly on the spot. He drinks with his intimates a beverage which is concocted of millet laced with honey ... Their religion is king-worship, believing that it is they who bring life and death, sickness and health.

He also tells us of the people:

Their cattle are goats and cows, camels and horses. Millet chiefly is cultivated in their land, and beans, also wheat. Most of the ordinary people go naked, covering themselves with skins. They spend their time cultivating and looking after their cattle.

About A.D. 800 the Kanuri emerge as a distinct people, with a king and their own land. They settled to the east of Lake Chad, and according to legend, the first of their kings was Dugu. The lists of kings in the Bornu Chronicle, which is the written history of Kanem-Bornu (though some of it was written very much later from carefully memorized traditional stories), give a number of pagan rulers between 800 and 1085, when the first Muslim ruler, Houmé, came to the throne. Again from the Chronicle of Bornu, we learn that the capital of Kanem was a town called Njimi, but as yet we do not know exactly where this was. Much of it must have consisted of the simple settlements typical of semi-nomadic peoples – reed huts, thatched roofs, nothing that leaves traces for us to find – but tradition has it that a red brick palace was built,

69

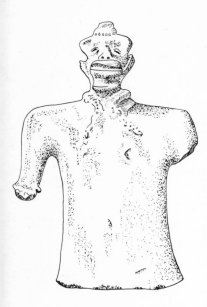

So funerary statuette.

and as there are many red brick ruins in Kanem, it is possible that one of them may yet be identified as the palace of Njimi. Red brick was an innovation, and had perhaps been introduced by builders from the Nile, where it was fairly common, but it was an important advance in the arts of civilization. Horses and camels were introduced in large numbers by the Kanuri at this time, and they put their horses to good use, for their cavalry became a source of terror to other peoples and was the main military force of the kings. It was renowned from the Nile to the Niger, right across Africa.

During the next 150 years, Kanem became more and more powerful, and developed a form of government which was similar to that of Ghana, Mali or Songhai, with a ruling house loosely controlling a number of tribute-paying peoples, and taking the responsibility for carving out their states' progress in the Sudan world. Under King Salma, (1194–1221) Islam became more firmly established as the religion of Kanem; mosques were built, and it is said that a learned Muslim religious leader read 150 books with Salma's son. So Kanem became a part of the Islamic world, and was able to enjoy the benefits which this unity implied; and also the benefits of reading and writing and contact with Arab learning and civilization. King Salma began to make wars of conquest using his feared cavalry, and during the reign of the next king, Dunama Dabbalemi, Kanem gained control of the whole of the Chad basin, and of the trade routes as far north as Fezzan, and made contact with the rulers of Tunis. This was of great importance for the country's trade, for it meant that caravans could journey safely far south from the Mediterranean coast, bringing with them much needed goods. Kanuri trade was mostly in slaves, and they were keen to acquire horses in return, though they imported manufactured goods from the North as well. Dunama Dabbalemi is referred to by Arab writers as King of Kanem and Lord of Bornu, and in his own country he was the 'Mai' or king. Kanem reached the peak of its fortunes during this king's reign, and over the next hundred years it became weakened by wars and royal quarrels.

The Kanuri were not left in peace to control their lands, and there were perpetual wars and revolts, from the So in the west and the Bulala in the east in particular. To add to these difficulties, there was much quarrelling within the royal house and many rival

70

The King of Bornu giving audience. (From Denham and Clapperton: *Narrative of Travels in Central Africa.*) (See also caption, page 73).

claimants to the throne of Kanem. The power of the country was reduced by so much fighting and raiding, and most of all perhaps by the lack of peace in which to grow prosperous. At the end of the fourteenth century, about 1386, Mai Omar found that he could no longer hold his lands against the Bulala, and he and many of his people moved to the west of Lake Chad and settled there. They remained there, and their new lands became the kingdom of Bornu.

In Bornu, there lived a settled agricultural population, whose daily lives were not much altered by the descent of the Kanuri upon them, for, as was usual their own chiefs and elders were left to use their customary authority. The Kanuri Mai divided up the country into provinces and estates, making gifts of pieces of land to those of his ministers whom he wished to reward, and in time of war each estate owner provided from the men living on his land. The Mai continued to live in a god-like manner, and was never seen by the people, interviews being given from behind a curtain or screen. Wars and raiding continued, and it was not until the reign of Mai Ali, who ruled from 1476–1507, that Bornu settled down and began to prosper.

As a first sign of prosperity, Ali built a new capital city at Birni Gazargamo on the river Yobé, which lasted until it was captured by the Fulani in 1811. The ruins of Gazargamo can be seen today, in northern Bornu, on the frontier between Nigeria and the Republic of Niger. They are surrounded by an immense earth wall, still about 20 feet high, which encloses a roughly circular area about $1\frac{3}{4}$ miles across. There was a large and elaborate palace of red brick, and various other red brick buildings, but the greater part of the enclosure must have contained houses of less durable material, sun-dried brick or reed huts, for few traces of them remain. The outer wall had five entrances, probably great gateways which now appear only as gaps in the wall, and a depression marking a defensive ditch outside the great wall can still be seen. These ruins make an impressive monument, and Gazargamo may well have been the largest African town of its time.

In 1570, the most famous of the kings of Bornu, Idris Aloma, came to the throne. He is known chiefly for his campaigns, because the chief of his religious leaders wrote an account of his wars.

By this time, the army of Bornu would have looked most distinctive, mounted on horses, wearing chain mail, quilted armour and

iron helmets, a type of military clothing which was later to spread from the area of Chad eastwards to the Nile. The army was introduced to the use of firearms, which Idris had discovered when on a pilgrimage early in his reign, and Turkish military instructors were employed to teach the handling of them. So firearms were in use in Bornu a few years before Judar and his desert army used them with such devastating effect on the Songhai, in 1591. With such an army behind him, Idris subdued all his neighbours, attacked and defeated Tuareg tribes, and re-conquered Kanem, where the Bulala, who had originally driven the Kanuri out, had settled. He made an agreement with the Bulala, allowing them to remain independent, and for the only time in the history of this part of Africa, a frontier between two kingdoms was carefully marked, though it does not seem that much notice was taken of it. Prisoners of war were sold for slaves. This was the trade on which Bornu based her prosperity, though it never brought as much wealth to Bornu as the gold trade gave to the states of the Western Sudan. With all these wars, Idris did not make any great extensions to the size of his kingdom, but he ensured peace within its boundaries by subduing the tribute paying peoples which Bornu

A soldier wearing the quilted clothing used by the army of Bornu.
The Bodyguard of the King of Bornu.

These two pictures, and that on page 71, were drawn by travellers in the early nineteenth century. (*From Denham & Clapperton: 'Narrative of Travels in Central Africa'*.)

controlled – he must have struck fear into their hearts with his swashbuckling horsemen – and secured his kingdom from outside attack by fighting potential raiders, such as the Tuareg.

He tried to unite his own people further by making Islam the state religion. Hitherto, although the ruling family and the important people of the ruling class had been Muslims for a long time, the ordinary people had not been greatly affected and had maintained their own customs and beliefs, which, you will remember, had also been the case in Ghana, Mali and Songhai. Now in Bornu, Idris built many mosques, and encouraged his people to go on the pilgrimage by building a special hostel for them in Mecca; but perhaps what had the most immediate effect on them was the introduction of Muslim law. This took the place of their own customary law, and the administering of the new law was handed over to the *qadis*, the Muslim judges.

In these ways Idris Aloma made Bornu the most powerful of the states of the Central Sudan, and when he died, having been killed by a blow from an iron hoe on one of his raiding expeditions, he left a well-established kingdom, with a character of its own, a warrior's kingdom with an aristocratic army, magnificent in its pageantry and pomp.

When Europeans, such as Heinrich Barth, first visited Bornu in the first half of the last century, much of this medieval splendour was still to be seen, and Barth gives a vivid account of the colour and pageantry which he saw. Indeed anyone who has been fortunate enough to see one of the mounted displays which the people of Bornu still give, when the horses and their riders are dressed in brightly coloured clothes of the old design, and when they charge brandishing their spears and swords, their pennants flying, their tassels dancing in the dust, will know how this splendour survives still, and moreover will have a good idea of how the armies of Bornu must have appeared in days long gone.

Urvoy, a French scholar, who is famous for his work on Bornu, wrote: 'Kanem ... Mali ... and Ghana were the centres which saw the elaboration of Sudanese civilization as we know it today, so different from the civilization of the Arabs and from that of the more purely African tribes of the south'. Kanem and Bornu exerted the same civilizing influence on the central Sudan as Ghana, Mali and Songhai had done in the west.

75

Modern Bornu horsemen dressed in colourful clothes similar to those of their forefathers.

6. The Forest States

THE equatorial forest stretches right across the middle of Africa, almost from one coast to the other. The change in scenery could hardly be more striking, from desert land or savannah to the lush thick vegetation of the forests, from a mainly dry climate to one where rain is frequent and heavy. There were no known travellers to this part of Africa before the arrival of the Europeans, that is to say none who wrote of their travels, so that before the fifteenth century there is no written information about the people who lived here, and few travellers went inland from the coast until the nineteenth century. The forest lay beyond the travels of the Arabs whose writings have been so useful to us in studying the history of the states of the Sudan; though, as we have seen, they would have liked to find the gold mines which lay within the forest area. In fact the mystery of the forest lands was such that all kinds of fantastic stories were made up about the people who lived there, enough to frighten off any intending traveller in search of gold mines, as may perhaps have been the object of these stories.

Since we have no written records, we must rely on archaeological work and on the traditional stories of the various peoples—'oral tradition' – for our information, and as yet there are few facts. Archaeological work has only recently begun, and oral tradition, though extremely valuable, cannot be relied upon to produce undoubted historical facts.

THE NOK CULTURE

The earliest culture of this part of West Africa which has so far been discovered is one from the central Nigerian plateau. It has been called the Nok culture, named after the village, near Jos, where it was first discovered. In the course of tin-mining operations, some life-like heads of baked clay, *terra cotta*, were found, and later many similar heads and parts of statues were found at

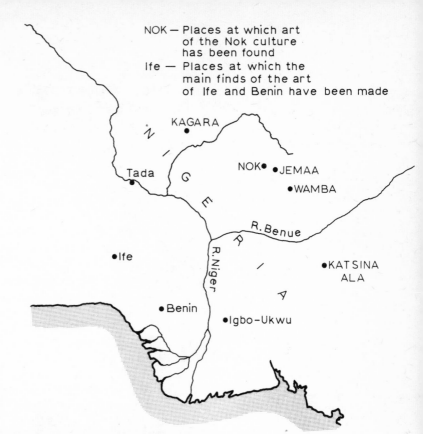

NOK — Places at which art
of the Nok culture
has been found

Ife — Places at which the
main finds of the art
of Ife and Benin have been made

KAGARA

Tada

NOK ● ● JEMAA

● WAMBA

R. Benue

● Ife

R. Niger

● KATSINA
ALA

● Benin

● Igbo-Ukwu

Map of Nigeria showing the main
centres at which examples of the
famous art of Nok, Ife and Benin
have been found.

other places as well. These heads are mostly quite small, but a
few of them are almost life size. They are not mere sketches of a
human head but are well modelled, and some of them could almost
be portraits of particular people. It is interesting to note that there
are marked resemblances between them and the well-known heads
of Benin and Ife, and the modelling of the eyes is very similar to
that of modern Yoruba art. It may be that the people of Nok were
the fathers of a tradition of art which has been carried on in western
Nigeria until the present day. We know very little about them, but
other of their possessions have been found as well as the heads,
for example, stone hoes, which show that they practised agriculture, and an iron axehead. From the evidence of these objects and
from scientific tests which have been carried out, it has been
suggested that the Nok culture existed from about 900 B.C. to
about A.D. 200, though these dates cannot be precise, and this
culture may have been somewhat later.

77

Terra cotta head from Nok. (*Bernard Fagg*.)

THE YORUBA

The Yoruba states were probably the largest and most important of the forest states, and certainly lasted the longest. Some of the forest peoples have in their legends a tradition that they came from the East, and amongst these are the Yoruba. This belief is of long standing, and in an early Arabic book we can read of the 'sons of Kush' who marched westward across the Nile, and of whom some turned 'rightward, between east and west, but the others, very numerous, marched towards the setting sun'. The latter would be the ones who are supposed to have reached the 'West' Coast. Some scholars have seen support for this legend in the likenesses between things in Egypt and things in West Africa, but this need not point to a long trek from the east by the whole Yoruba people. It is more likely that if people from the east did come amongst them, they were the same kind as those who settled in Kanem, warriors who settled amongst the peaceful agricultural population they found there, and set about organizing them into a distinct group. There is, however, no real evidence to suggest that the Yoruba ever lived in any part of Africa other than the western area where they still live.

An ivory leopard inlaid with copper, from Benin.

Although we think of the Yoruba as forest dwellers, they have not always been so. Oyo, one of the chief Yoruba states, lies beyond the northern edge of the forest and in medieval days used cavalry in its army. Horsemen would be at a great disadvantage trying to move about in the forest and this suggests that they were in contact with the states of the Sudan – probably the Hausa states and Kanem as they were the nearest. Ife, the great centre of Yoruba culture, is situated near the edge of the forest, and was probably subject to the same influences – as also was Benin, which was an offshoot of Ife, but further south.

The culture of Ife and Benin is probably the most famous of all the old civilizations of the African Forest. It has become widely known in the world from the discoveries of the magnificent art practised in these towns for hundreds of years. Bronze and brass heads and statuettes were found in Benin by the British Military Expedition in 1897, and were taken to Europe, and later a European traveller, Frobenius, discovered others at Ife in 1910. These heads are much admired and are ranked amongst the great art of the world; indeed they are of a style which had not been seen

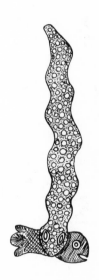

A snake catching a fish.

The Oni (ruler) of Ife wearing a bead crown and plume. This head is thought to have been made between the twelfth and fourteenth centuries. (*British Museum.*)

before, of excellent workmanship and great beauty. Some of the finest of them are thought to have been made in the fourteenth century and to portray the heads of rulers. As archaeological work proceeds in Nigeria, more of these works of art are being found – further finds at Ife, and a new collection from Igbo-Ukwu near Enugu are examples of recent discoveries. Whether the Yoruba and other peoples of Nigeria learned the art of this complicated method of bronze casting from others, or not, is not known, though it was practised in other places, as for example in Ancient Egypt, but even if anyone taught them the *method*, there is no doubt that the art and style were distinctly their own inspiration.

We do not know very much about the Yoruba of those times, but they lived in big walled cities at least as early as A.D. 1300, and cultivated fields which lay outside the walls. They engaged in trade with the states to the north, exchanging cloth and kola nuts for the goods they wanted. After the sixteenth century they began to look south rather than north for their trade, for Benin and Lagos had become important trading centres with the arrival of Europeans by sea. By this time Benin, which earlier had been conquered by the Yoruba, had become a state itself, and Benin city was the centre for a wide area of which Lagos, hitherto independent, became a part. Europeans came here to buy ivory, pepper, and slaves, and were impressed with its size, its wide streets and neat rows of houses. A Dutch visitor, in 1602, describes it as a walled town, and says the main street was about four miles long. He also described the king's palace, commenting on its wide rooms, its galleries and courtyards and the great brass figures which decorated it; 'Wherever I looked', he says, 'still I saw gates upon gates to go into other places!' He saw the king's horses in their stables, and the king's slaves carrying water, yams, and palm-wine for their master, and much grass for his horses. Later, civil wars caused the decay of Benin as a place of much importance, and the rise of the Yoruba state of Oyo helped to bring about its downfall. By the end of the seventeenth century, Benin was much reduced; parts of the city were deserted and crumbled into ruin, and slave raiding by the armies of Benin had removed so many people from the surrounding country that much cultivated land fell into disuse. Benin became a shadow of its former self, the earlier greatness of the city a memory.

The Yoruba state of Oyo was a small state on the northern

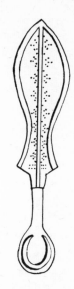

A ceremonial sword from Benin.

Decoration of a fish, a favourite symbol of the metal workers of Benin.

The City of Benin in the seventeenth century. This picture is taken from the book of a Dutch geographer, Olphert Dapper (1668). The building with the two spires, each of which has a bird on top of it, is the Palace. The King himself is riding the horse in the foreground of the picture.

edge of the forest until about the end of the sixteenth century, when developing trade on the coast attracted it to turn to the south rather than northward to the Sudan for its trade, as had been its custom. Oyo was some way from the coast, and the Yoruba had to conquer a way to the sea, pushing gradually far away to the south-west and taking into their empire a part of Dahomey. They did not reach the sea and actually owned no ports but they used those where Yoruba were settled such as Lagos and Badagri. Their power and prosperity increased, based mainly on the trade in slaves, for by now this was at its height. At the peak of its power, Oyo received tribute from places as far apart as Nupe and Borgu in the North, to parts of Dahomey in the west, and as far as Benin's borders in the east, and was politically the most powerful of all the Yoruba states, though Ife seems always to have maintained its position as the centre of Yoruba culture and religion. Oyo enjoyed a period of wealth and power but ultimately the tribute paying peoples became discontented because of the tyranny of the Yoruba, and because the wealth which they helped to gain seemed to benefit them very little. Wars, defection and revolts during the eighteenth century and into the nineteenth brought Oyo to such a state of disorder that it ceased to be of any political importance.

82

A bronze horseman, from Benin. (*British Museum*.)   A small ivory carving of exceptionally fine workman-ship, also from Benin. (*British Museum*.)

THE AKAN OF ASHANTI

Like the Yoruba, the Akan people also have a tradition of a long journey from distant places in their early history. This time it is from the North that they believe they came, from the lands near the River Niger, perhaps about 600 years ago, and founded an ancient capital at Bono Mansu, about 72 miles north of their modern capital at Kumasi. Bono Mansu lay in orchard bush beyond the northern limits of the forest, and grew rich on trade with the states of the Sudan. It is likely that this legend refers to the coming of a northern people who moved in and settled amongst the Akan speakers whom they found already living in the area. This happened probably during the fourteenth century, and in the next century there was further movement from the north directly into the forest areas. A number of small Akan states grew up, but those in the north remained the strongest, though their position was challenged by Denkyera in the central forest area, to whom many of the smaller forest states had been forced to pay tribute.

This was happening during the seventeenth century, and later pressure from another group of Akan, who were pushing in from the west, the Doma, caused several of the states round Kumasi, who had been paying tribute to Denkyera, to join together to make a stand against the invasion of their lands. At the end of the seventeenth century, under Osei Tutu, the king of Kumasi, and his chief priest Okomfo Anokye, the allied states succeeded in defeating the Doma and driving them off.

The states of Ashanti, Oyo and Benin.

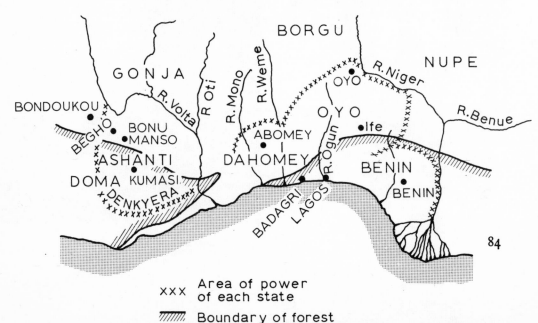

xxx Area of power of each state

/////// Boundary of forest

84

After this success, Osei Tutu set to work with great diplomacy to weld his allies into a unified body, a nation which would have the strength of a common purpose which at that moment was the defeat of the pushful Denkyera state. The traditional stories of the Akan people tell us that Osei Tutu called a great meeting to which the leaders of his allies came, and that after discussion, a stool of gold came down from the sky to rest on Osei Tutu's knees. This was accepted by everyone present as the embodiment of a united spirit amongst all their states, and they pledged their support for it, and swore allegiance to it. Osei Tutu became the Asantehene, the leader of the people of Ashanti, for all the small states banded together and called themselves the Ashanti Union. The Stool became the symbol of the spirit of the Ashanti nation, and all health and power were embodied in it. The safety of the Stool meant the safety of the nation.

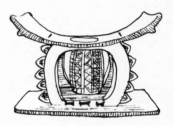

An Ashanti stool.

With this new power behind him, Osei Tutu decided that the time had come to deal with the Denkyera, and so, when their king sent for his annual tribute, the messenger who brought the demand was killed by one of the Ashanti chiefs – it is said, by the chief of Juaben. Such daring gave cause for war, and the two armies met not far from Kumasi. Denkyera was defeated, and the Union proceeded to conquer other states to the south, toward the profitable trade of the coast, and by the early nineteenth century it had become the most powerful and important state in the area, its prosperity being built on the flourishing coastal trade in slaves and gold.

Before this time, however, there must have been a steady trade northwards. Undoubtedly merchants came from the states to the north, from Mali in particular, in pursuit of trade. In Twi, the language of the Akan peoples, there are words which are borrowed from Mande, the main language of Mali – words which were used in commerce such as those for goods exchanged, tobacco, snuff, slaves, or gold; for containers, such as box, sack, pouch; for transport such as horse and camel; and there were other words as well. Some Mande-speaking peoples in the area of Bondouku have a traditional story that they once lived in a town called Begho, which stretches across a gap in the Banda Hills. Its ruins are still to be seen in the shape of high grass-covered mounds, and tradition tells us that it was a town in two parts, like ancient Ghana, with one part largely Muslim, and the other inhabited by

85

A mosque in northern Ghana.

Gold mask of King Kofi Karikari.
(*Wallace Collection.*)

the local people. Here gold and kola nuts were collected, probably not just from the area round Begho, but from further south as well. Begho was no doubt a collecting point for the northern trade, and the starting place for caravans to the north, which followed a route to Jenné on the Niger. An account of this trade written in 1679 says that the Mande traders would not allow the forest traders to enter the town of Begho at all; they had to carry on their trade in the bush outside the town 'which is called the market', and where the old 'silent' trade was practised. It is likely that Begho was in existence as a trading centre long before 1679, however, and was probably supplying Jenné with gold at least as early as the fourteenth and fifteenth centuries, when that town was at the height of its importance.

There were Muslim traders in many of the towns and markets of Ashanti, never so many as seriously to influence or to affect the life of the Akan people, but enough to form a definite community. To some extent they were encouraged, no doubt with the idea of keeping up continuing trade with the north, which must therefore have been considered important. In the latter part of the eighteenth century, when Opoku II was Asantehene, he ordered that Muslims taken prisoner in battle should be neither killed nor sold into slavery, as was the usual fate of prisoners, and had them 'distributed amongst the provinces and the capital'. So little communities of Muslims, settled in the markets of Ashanti, gave that kingdom a flavour of the north, and brought it into the fringes of the Islamic world.

Ashanti brass weights, used for weighing gold dust.

The extent to which the Akan peoples were affected by more northerly peoples is not known to us; it is too far back in history for there to be any reliable tradition, and there is little evidence in writing so far, though more is being discovered each year in the form of manuscripts written in Arabic. These have sometimes been carefully kept for up to 200 years and their discovery and translation is opening new paths into the history of this part of Africa. Excavation of ancient towns such as Bono Mansu and Begho would tell us more, and would also give an indication of the size, wealth and importance of these cities.

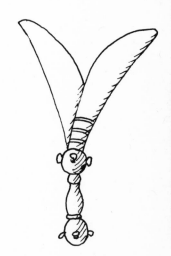

A ewer (jug) of the English King Richard II (1367–1400) was found at Kumasi towards the end of the last century. It would be interesting to know how it came there – possibly by sea in the hands of a trader who exchanged it on the coast for the goods he wanted; but perhaps it made the long journey overland after crossing the Mediterranean – for Richard was often in France – and passed from hand to hand along the caravan routes until it finally became part of a treasured hoard in Kumasi.

The ewer of Richard II found at Kumasi. (*British Museum*.)

THE PEOPLES OF THE CONGO

Our knowledge of the history of this part of Africa is very sparse, and much of it is due to the interest of a particular scholar in some problems so that there are some things of which we may have a fair knowledge, and others, equally important, of which we know very little. It is clear, however, from what is already known, that in this part of Africa there were medieval states which were well run and had the benefit of central government and organization.

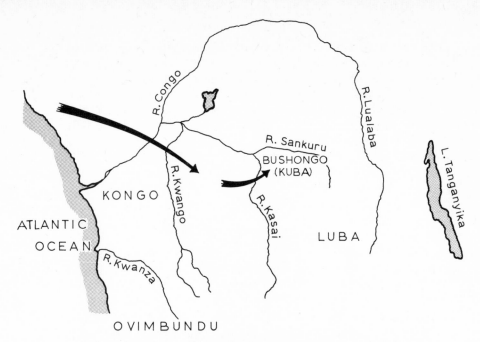

South of the Congo River, the forest comes to an end and savannah land takes its place, with long grasses in the plains and rivers with tree-shaded banks. It is easy to move about in, and the land is fertile enough for crop growing. One of the peoples who lived in this part were the Kuba, who came originally from the area now called Gabon, about the middle of the west coast of Africa. When the Portuguese arrived on the coast towards the end of the fifteenth century, the Kuba fled eastwards and settled near the Kwango River where they lived in small communities and gained a livelihood from hunting and fishing. Here they stayed until sometime in the first half of the seventeenth century when the raids of other warlike tribes decided them to move on again, and they went further east to a stretch of country between the Kasai and Sankuru rivers.

This last move was a permanent one, and it was here that a state grew up which was outstanding in many respects. What we know of the history of the Kuba is based largely on the patient work of historians who have studied their traditional stories. We learn from them that the Kuba settled down amongst the people they found already living in the area they had chosen, and continued with their familiar way of life, hunting and fishing, for a time,

89

and, as we shall see, they ultimately grew into a powerful state. We do not know very much about how they lived in these early days, but beyond hunting and fishing, they began to practise crop growing, a skill which they believe they learned from the people amongst whom they settled, and cultivated bananas and millet. They wore clothes made of bark cloth – a soft pliable material made by carefully stripping the bark from trees and beating it with little hammers – and also made things from raffia, a kind of dried grass. Even today, the descendants of these people are famous for their weaving of raffia and other dried plants, and the walls of their houses are sometimes made of beautifully patterned mats. They used iron and copper tools, bringing the metals from the mines of the Lower Congo.

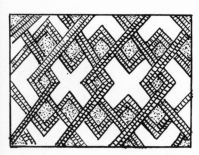

A Bushongo raffia pattern.

Up till this time, the Kuba had been divided, socially, into small groups, each one of which had a chief or leader, and during their last move one of these groups, the Bushongo, had chosen from among their group a 'captain of canoes', who, because of his importance amongst a fishing people, became powerful. Once settled, the 'captain of canoes' became king, though in the early days of this new organization, he was no more than an acknowledged leader. He was elected by a council of all the chiefs, and if they came to dislike or distrust him for some reason, he could be deposed. However, it was not long before the leader became more king-like, and all the things which we associate with kingship developed – a royal family from which a whole line of kings would ascend the throne; a state ceremonial; and the swearing of loyalty and support for the king by the chiefs of the other groups, each of whom presented him with a wife as a token of their allegiance, and to ensure his interest in them. A state with a central government was built out of the separate small groups into which the Kuba had previously been divided, and it took the name of the group which had become the most important, the Bushongo. Councils were formed to deal with social and political matters, and officials were appointed by the king and given titles, rather as Ministers are appointed today. A system of collecting tribute or taxes was developed, and the whole area where the Kuba had settled became a unified state.

Sometime in the earlier part of the seventeenth century there came to power a man who made a lasting name for himself. This was King Shamba Bolongongo, who was not of the original royal

Carved statue in wood of King
Shamba Bolongongo, said to have
been made in his lifetime. (*Eliot
Elisofon.*)

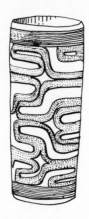

A carved wooden cup.

A carved wooden drum.

house, nor even of that branch of the Kuba of whom we have been learning. He came from a different branch of the Kuba which invaded the Bushongo states between the rivers, killed the King, and destroyed the capital. Even so, Shamba Bolongongo, though he usurped the throne and forced himself on the Bushongo, became respected and revered by them. A famous Belgian scholar, Emile Torday, who spent much of his life studying this part of Africa and collecting the traditional stories of the people, wrote of Shamba Bolongongo early in the present century: 'A Central African King of the early days of the seventeenth century whose only conquests were in the field of thought, public prosperity, and social progress, and who is still remembered in our day by every person in the country . . . must have been a remarkable man indeed'. There is some truth in this, for Shamba made various changes which strengthened his kingdom. For a start, he encouraged so many people to live in his capital city that he was certain of having plenty of men for his army without further trouble. So strong was this army that the small states surrounding the Bushongo lands were fearful of opposing Shamba, and consequently were brought under his control, one by one, and incorporated into his kingdom. He employed the same kind of control over them which we have seen in the Sudan states – an indirect rule in which the subdued peoples were allowed to continue with their own way of life, and kept their own rulers, but had obligations to the central power of the state which meant the paying of tribute and taxes, and giving whatever help and support was asked of them.

Shamba Bolongongo then built up the prosperity of his state. Before he came there, he had been living further west in an area where various skills and crops brought in by the Portuguese were used. Maize, groundnuts and tomatoes, which the Portuguese had imported from America, were amongst the new crops which Shamba introduced to his people. It is said that he also taught them wood carving and the weaving of cloth; skilled artists set to work, and in wood carving particularly they excelled, producing carvings which compare well with the great art of Benin and Ife. Trade flourished, and by the end of the seventeenth century the Bushongo were moving far afield, over country to the south of the Congo, as far east as the Lualaba River, westwards almost to the coast, and southwards to the Ovimbundu people who lived south of the Kwanza River. All this brought them into touch with other cultures and ideas. With peaceful conditions at home, prosperity, and the support of a state which had well-organized political and legal systems, the Bushongo were able to develop a civilization of their own, using what pleased them of other peoples' ideas, weaving them in with their own, so that there emerged a culture which was distinctive and of a high standard.

The Bushongo are only one of several states with a similar history and achievement in this part of Africa, but they are probably the best known, partly because of their famous wood carvings, and partly because of the amount of research which has been done to find out about their history. Many other peoples are known from the fragments of pottery which archaeologists turn up or from traditional stories, but as yet little can be said about them. So far as is at present known, the Bushongo appear to have been rather less influenced by outside cultures than many other African peoples were, and the fact that they were able to develop such an organized state largely out of their own experience is a point of particular interest.

A wooden box in the form of a crocodile.

THE PEOPLE OF UGANDA

The last of the forest or semi-forest peoples with whom we shall deal are the peoples of the modern state of Uganda. Uganda lies to the east of the main forest area, and while there is some forest there, it covers only a small extent of land. In the main, Uganda is a fertile country with good pastures and cultivable land; it is well watered by rivers and great lakes; and there are high mountains, such as Ruwenzori, and much hilly country in the west. Oral tradition again is our main source of information, for here there are no written records. The first European came to Uganda only about a hundred years ago, and though Arab and Swahili traders (people from the East Coast of Africa) had travelled as far inland as the shores of Lake Victoria some years earlier, they left no record of

93

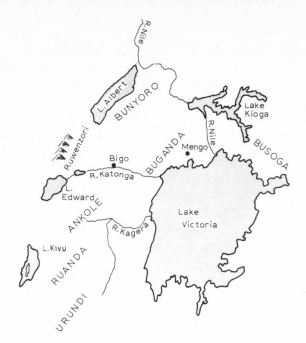

The states round Lake Victoria.

their journeys, difficult and dangerous though they may have been. They were hunting for slaves and ivory to sell on the coast, and kept no diaries.

Tradition makes it clear that the most powerful of the peoples of that area, the Baganda and Banyoro, came into existence as distinct communities sometime during the late middle ages. They are now a Bantu-speaking people, and it is believed that they came from the north to settle in the fertile valleys beside the lakes. It is likely that originally they were a military group speaking a different language who conquered the people they found already on the land, a peaceful, agricultural population in all probability, and imposed their rule on them. Then, intermarrying with the conquered, they gradually adopted their Bantu language. Each would take something from the culture of the other until a unified people grew out of the welding of the two.

Ancient stories tell us that a mythical people called the Bacwezi were the ancestors not only of the ruling house of Buganda, one of the four states which exist today in Uganda, but also of many other rulers of those parts. In these stories the Bacwezi are a race of giants who accomplish miraculous feats, and while we cannot believe in the exact truth of these stories, there is no doubt that the people existed, and that they came from the north. It is possible that the Bahima, a tall brown-skinned cattle-owning people, are the descendants of the Bacwezi. Nowadays they travel the plains and pastures with their cattle, their most precious possessions whose welfare and comfort are the most important thing to a Bahima tribesman. They live in grass huts in a circular village, the cattle being protected from harm by living in the open centre surrounded by a 'wall' of huts. When the pasture grows scarce in a particular place they move on, deserting the village they have built. Such ancient monuments as there are in Uganda were traditionally built by the Bacwezi, and were built at least partly for the protection of cattle in time of war, and it is for this reason that a possible connection between the Bacwezi and the Bahima has been suggested.

Whatever the truth may be, there is no doubt that people with ideas of military and social organization came into the country at least five hundred years ago, and were the builders of the fortified camps which are spread through the country. These camps are great earthworks consisting of an arrangement of defensive ditches surrounding an area to be protected, which often had a mound in

Modern Bahima and their cattle.

An iron arrowhead of the type used by Bahima for piercing the necks of cattle.

the centre. The trenches are cut into the rock underlying the surface earth, and the people who made them must have had good and useful tools. At Bigo, the largest of the camps, where some archaeological excavation has been done, the ditches were found to form a very good defence against an enemy, while the central area which they protected, which was over a mile across and of oval shape, contained a mound which gave a very good view over the surrounding country. These forts were certainly built for defence, but they are too big to have been meant simply for a military garrison and must have been intended for the safety of a tribal group, including families and their cattle. Examples of a special kind of iron arrowhead used for piercing the neck of cattle to draw blood were found at Bigo, and it is certain that these animals were kept there, and likely that the size of the enclosure was for their benefit. Many theories have been put forward in the past as to who may have built these huge monuments; Portuguese, Abyssinians, even, by some wild flight of the imagination, the ancient Romans, have all been suggested, but there is no doubt that they were built by an African people very similar to the present inhabitants, if they were not their direct forebears.

What happened in the four main kingdoms of Uganda before the arrival of Europeans is known only from the stories which each kingdom has preserved, carefully memorized and handed on from

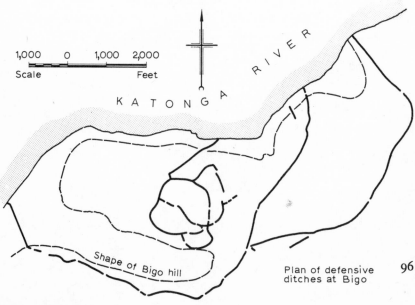

Plan of the defensive ditches at Bigo.

Excavating at Bigo.

generation to generation. Much of this memory is concerned with lists of kings' names and the names of their families, but where accounts of actual events have been passed on, they vary so much from place to place that it is difficult even to guess at the truth. However, some facts stand out which give a general picture of what was happening.

During the seventeenth century, the Banyoro seem to have been the first to become powerful, and their warriors were sent on raids towards the south-west, among the people of Ankole and Urundi, who were much the same as themselves. They also raided eastwards into Buganda, and beyond it into Busoga. They must have been well organized, from a military point of view, to carry their raids over such a wide area. In the eighteenth century, the Baganda retaliated and raided in their turn, overrunning Busoga, attacking the Banyoro and conquering pieces of their territory which have been part of Buganda ever since. The Baganda became the most powerful of all these people, and have remained so until the present day.

Once the Europeans arrived in this part of Africa, we are immediately in the world of reports, diaries and written records; and these throw light on the society which they met and the conditions

97

Bark cloth hammer, of bone.

under which it lived. The first European to visit Uganda was John Hanning Speke, an English explorer, who arrived in 1862, and he tells us what he found. Somewhat to his surprise, he found an organized state, with a king called then, as now, the 'Kabaka', who was assisted by a council of chiefs in the ruling of his kingdom. The king was elected by the council normally from the sons of the previous king, and those sons who failed to be elected were usually imprisoned or put to death to avoid the possibility of fighting and rebellion amongst rival claimants to the throne and their supporters. The members of the council were appointed by the king and had special duties such as the administration of a particular area; the *Mujasi* had charge of the army; the *Gabunga* controlled the war-canoes; while some held slightly less important posts such as the chief brewer, or the keeper of the drums. These officials were expected always to be at court at the service of the king, though administrators naturally were allowed to spend time controlling their provinces too. Court manners were laid down and had to be most strictly observed, for the king was regarded as a god, and in spite of his council of ministers, he had to be treated as such, so that his word was absolute, his decision law. This is how Speke describes King Mutesa whom he visited in his hill-top palace at Mengo not far from the modern city of Kampala:

> The king was a good looking, well-figured, tall young man of twenty-five. He sat on a red blanket spread upon a square platform of royal grass and was scrupulously well dressed in a raiment of new bark cloth. The hair of his head was cut short, except on top where it was combed into a high ridge. On his neck was a large ring of beautifully worked small beads. On one arm was another bead ornament, prettily devised, and on the other a wooden charm tied by a string covered with a snakeskin. On every finger and every toe he had alternate brass and copper rings, and above the ankle a stocking of pretty beads. Everything was light, neat, and elegant.
>
> At his feet were the symbols of royalty, a spear, a shield, and a white dog.

The state was rich, deriving its wealth from the trade in slaves, but this only became a really big source of revenue from about 1840 onwards when the Arab slave dealers first visited Uganda. It was said that Mutesa kept an army of 6000 men continually on

98

A typical Baganda hut made of cane, with a thatched roof. (*Crown Copyright.*)

The king of Bunyoro receiving gifts on his jubilee. (*Crown Copyright.*)

the hunt for slaves which he then exchanged with the Arab dealers, mostly for firearms. By 1872, he was renowned for his ownership of 1000 guns.

The Baganda lived in unusual and attractive huts made out of dried stalks from the long reeds which grow in the lakes and rivers like the papyrus, and these dried stalks were woven into round shaped buildings with conical roofs, slightly overhanging the walls, and were light, cool, and shady in the hot weather, yet offered protection from the rain. All the royal tombs are enclosed in this kind of hut, and they are characteristic only of this part of Africa. They wore clothing made of bark cloth, which they made using wood, bone or ivory hammers to beat the bark into a pliable and durable material, and they knew how to make sandals; they also wore skins as additional clothing, cow, goat, antelope or colobus monkey, but not the leopard skin which was another symbol of royalty and the royal house alone might wear it. They made basket ware and pottery, iron tools, musical instruments – harps, drums and horns; and they made long canoes for travelling on the lakes, sometimes as much as 60 or 70 feet long. They cultivated bananas and plantains, which, when served with a sauce, formed their main foodstuff.

The states of Uganda, like that of the Bushongo, appear to have developed without much help from outside influences. Certainly they were not brought into the Islamic world, nor were they directly affected by non-Africans on the East Coast before the middle of the last century. There would inevitably have been an interchange of ideas, though, with other African peoples, particularly those further south, where natural barriers such as forest, mountain and swamp do not exist.

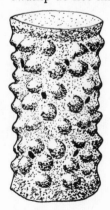

An unusual pot from Ntusi near Bigo; its purpose is unknown.

7. The Lands of the Zanj

WHEN the Portuguese sailed round the Cape of Good Hope some 500 years ago, they found to their surprise flourishing ports and coastal towns scattered along the coast of East Africa. Their journey had been to them, justifiably, a great adventure, an exploration into the unknown, and to find a civilization and towns as fine as many in Europe was quite unexpected. They found towns with tall, many-storeyed houses built of stone or coral, white and sparkling in the sun; harbours full of ships from other countries of the East, some of them larger and grander than their own, manned by sailors who knew their way across oceans unknown to the Portuguese, and had charts and instruments as good as theirs; a flourishing trade which gave these towns an air of settled prosperity and wealth, even luxury; and as the visitors looked about them and learned more of the land to which they had come, they realized that they had reached a world with wider, possibly wealthier, contacts in trade than their own. They were not treated as rare and distinguished guests, nor was their visit regarded as a particularly noteworthy event – the people of the coast were used to travellers by sea and were surprised only that the visitors had come from the south. The head of this expedition was Vasco da Gama, and the diary which he kept of his journey says: 'When we had been (there) two or three days, two gentlemen of the country came to see us. They were very haughty, and valued nothing that we gave them'. But the Portuguese 'cried with joy' at what they saw and heard about the country, for they saw it as a place in which to seek their own fortunes.

A long tradition of trading activities lay behind this prosperity. Roman coins, mostly of the third and fourth centuries A.D. have been found at various places along this coast, and are evidence of early visits, but even earlier than this a Greek pilot wrote a book for sailors to use called *The Periplus of the Erythraean Sea*. A 'Periplus'

The east African coast.

is a sailor's guide, giving all the information necessary for making a safe journey, and 'erythros' (from which 'Erythraean' comes) means 'red' in Greek, so that this book was a guide for sailors using the Red Sea. It also covered areas further south along the African coast as far south as a port called Rhapta (which is thought to have lain possibly between modern Dar-es-Salaam and Tanga), and the trade of the Indian Ocean. The book appeared about A.D. 110, and the writer was probably a Greek from Alexandria in Egypt. He may have known the coast south of the Red Sea himself, though his descriptions are more vague than the detailed information about the Red Sea harbours, and perhaps these were based on the experiences of other sailors. He tells us about the coastal voyage, breaking it up into convenient daily runs, listing the markets and ports of call, and giving each one a short description so that the seafarers would know what sort of people they would meet, and what could be bought or sold in the way of trade. At certain times of the year, the winds would blow the ships to the north-west Indian coast where 'wheat, rice, ghee, sesame oil, cotton cloth, girdles, and honey made from the reed called "sakchari" ' were collected. 'Some make their voyage directly to these market towns; others exchange cargo as they go.' From southern Arabia, the coastal towns of Kenya and Tanganyika, then called the country of Azania, imported the 'lances that are made made at Muza, especially for this trade, and hatchets, swords, and awls, and various kinds of glass; and at some places a little wine and wheat, but not for trade, but to obtain the goodwill of the inhabitants.' The goods exported from Azania were gold, rhinoceros horn, which was thought to have magical properties in the ancient world and was much sought after, tortoise shell, ivory and palm oil. According to the 'Periplus', the men of the coast were 'of piratical habits, very great in stature, and under separate chiefs for each place.' Each port was a small chiefdom at this time, and to the coast there came 'Arab captains and agents, who are familiar with the inhabitants and intermarry with them and who know the whole coast and understand the language.' They came in large ships, and knew the ways of the coastal people, and while all the organization of the trade was in the hands of the Arabs, the local people also played their part.

Who were the local people of this time? The writer of the 'Periplus' tells us interesting things about them but nowhere does

An Arab *dhow*, that is a sea-going ship used for trading from ancient times to the present day. (*Paul Popper.*)

he suggest that they were black or dark-skinned, and we learn of their appearance only that they were tall. A later writer, Claudius Ptolemy, who lived in the second century A.D., gives us a little more information. He wrote a *Geography* which is thought to have been edited after his death and published with some additions; and as it did not appear until the fourth century, it is likely that it represents all that was known in Egypt about geography by the fourth century. From Ptolemy we learn that dark-skinned people, perhaps Bantu-speaking, had begun to move into the coastal area, and he speaks of their presence at the southernmost part of the coastal strip, about as far north as the northern boundary of modern Mozambique. So by the fourth century it looks as though the Bantu-speaking people who now inhabit all this part of Africa were beginning to come in, perhaps from the west, from the land between the Zambesi and Congo rivers, though there is no certainty about this. From this time until about the tenth century there is little written information about the coast, though writers from other countries – Arabia, Persia, Indonesia, China – mention the black slaves who were brought from there. By the tenth century, according to the famous Arab geographer, Masudi, the whole coast was populated by a dark-skinned people as far north as the modern boundary between Kenya and Somaliland. The few words of their language which Masudi reports are much like Bantu, and it is likely that these were the ancestors of the modern people who live in this area.

We have seen the effect which the spread of Islam had on other parts of Africa, and here too it had an effect on events, though for slightly different reasons. The East African coast was used as a refuge by Muslims from Oman who had to flee their country as a result of an argument, which they lost, as to who was the rightful successor to the Prophet Mohammed. This was in the eighth century, according to tradition, and others who were in the same trouble followed from different parts of Arabia. There was probably not a very great number of refugees, but they settled on the coast and made their homes there, as well as on the islands. Later, according to traditional stories, they were joined by groups of Persians. There is the story of one of the later immigrants, Husain bin Ali, who, in 957, set sail from Shiraz with his six sons, each one with a ship in his charge. He had had a dream that a rat with a snout of iron was gnawing the town wall, and interpreted this to

Wooden lattice work fitted over the windows is typical of Arab architecture in the Red Sea area where this picture was taken.

mean that his country was going to be ruined. He and his sons set sail for the Swahili coast (as they called the east coast) and each of the ships founded a new settlement, amongst them such famous places as Mombasa, Pemba, and Kilwa. Here they became rulers, and their names are found in the written histories of these towns, though much of these histories is a record of traditional stories rather than events as they occurred, and the story of Husain and his sons may well not be strictly accurate.

Amongst the people who sailed from Oman was Masudi, the geographer whom we have mentioned before. He left Oman in A.D. 912 for the East African coast, travelling and studying to gain information for the book he was writing. This book appeared later with the exciting title of *The Meadows of Gold and the Mines of Gems*, meant, as Masudi says, to stir the imagination and make people eager to read history. He tells us about the coastal people, and it is interesting to notice that with all the information he gained (and he was determined to find out everything that he could) he makes little mention of anything happening inland from the coast, with one exception: this was inland from the port of Sofala, on the lower reaches of the Zambesi river, whence came gold from the mines of the land we now call Rhodesia.

By this time the coast was known as the Land of Zanj, 'Zanj'

A ruined Arab mansion in Lamu. (*From Elspeth Huxley: 'The Sorcerer's Apprentice' Chatto & Windus.*)

being the name which the Arabs gave to the coastal people. It survives now only in the name of the island of Zanzibar. From Masudi we learn that the coastal people were skilled in metal work, and used iron rather than silver or gold. They were hard working traders, and hunted the elephant for its tusks, though they made no use of the ivory themselves and wanted it only for trade. Ivory was much in demand in the Far East. Masudi says that the East Coast ivory was sent to Oman, and shipped thence to India and China, where it was used, in India, for making the hilts of swords and daggers, for scabbards, and for ornaments such as gaming pieces and chessmen. In China, it had a rather more spectacular use, for it was used to make splendid chairs in which kings, civil and military officials were carried – 'no officer or notable dares to come into the royal presence in an iron chair, and ivory alone can be used'. Tusks weighing fifty pounds and more were collected and exported for these purposes. The Zanj used oxen for beasts of burden and for war, we are told, and they were harnessed like horses and made to run as fast. Bananas, millet, meat, honey and coconuts were the main foodstuffs and a root called 'Kalari'; and, finally, the Zanj had an 'elegant language, and men who preach in it'.

106

Another writer, El Idrisi, who wrote an account of East Africa about 1154, shows how trade and prosperity had increased. Traders were now taking the coastal goods as far away as northern China, visiting Indonesia and Malaya, and calling at ports round the coast of India. The coastal towns and island harbours grew, Lamu, Malindi, Pemba, Kilwa, Sofala, Zanzibar and Mombasa. They were independent, each with its own ruler, but owed allegiance to the Arabs of southern Arabia in whose hands the organization of the commercial world remained. Idrisi says: 'The Zanj have no ships of their own to voyage in, but use vessels from Oman and other countries', so that they had to keep up their old relationship with these countries. They were exporting gold, iron, ivory, tortoise shell and slaves. Idrisi was particularly impressed with the trade in iron, and seemed to consider it more important than any other export, and the source of the largest profits. Indians came to the coast to buy iron and took it back to their own country where they re-sold it to manufacturers of iron weapons. He says the Zanj of Malindi owned and worked iron mines, as did other towns, but Malindi may have been the most important. The iron was much valued in India, partly because there was no lack of supply, and partly because it was of good quality yet easy to fashion, and they became masters in the skill of working it. The Indians were said to make better swords than anyone else, and weapons made of the iron of Zanj were used throughout the Middle East and countries of the Indian Ocean.

In exchange for the goods they exported, the coastal people bought a variety of things, many of which were luxuries, and point to the wealth and prosperity which by this time they had won. They bought Indian cloth and beads; and from further east came ships laden with precious pottery and porcelain from China, and stoneware, a kind of extra hard pottery, from Siam. The coast of East Africa is littered with fragments of this precious stuff, green, grey, brown, or the famous blue and white Ming porcelain, and this is some indication of the quantities which were brought in. Trade from the twelfth century until the arrival of the Portuguese at the end of the fifteenth must have been on a scale unknown in the rest of the world, and for the luxury of some of its imports, it must also have been outstanding. The Chinese themselves valued their pottery very highly, regarding each pot as an individual work of artistic creation, so that a skilled potter was a great artist, as

A Chinese blue and white porcelain bowl excavated at Gedi.

much so as a sculptor, a painter, or any other creator of valued works of art. A shipload of such pottery, even though much of it might not be of the highest class, must have represented a great deal of money, and its purchasers must have enjoyed a high standard of living. The more precious dishes were set into the walls of fine houses as decoration, and many were used for decorating the domed ceilings of mosques.

A description of Mombasa, written very early in the sixteenth century by a Portuguese, Duarte Barbosa, gives the impression of a fine city. 'There is a city of the Moors,' he says,

called Mombaça, very large and beautiful, and built of high and handsome houses of stone and whitewash, and with very

A map of Mombasa made by the Portuguese. (*British Museum.*)

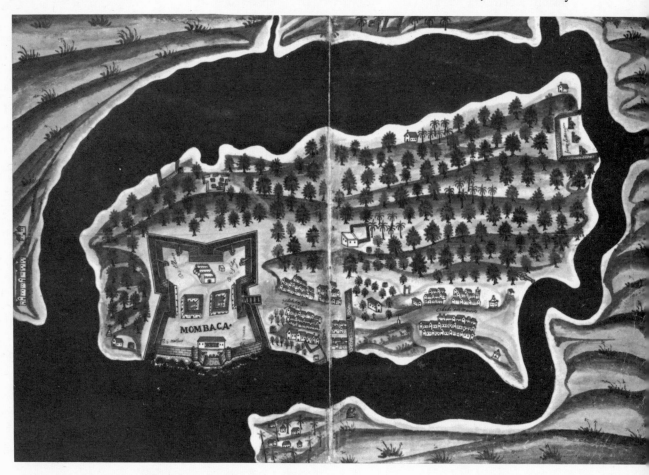

good streets . . . It has its own king, himself a Moor. The people are of dusky white and brown complexions, likewise the women who are bravely attired in silk and gold in abundance. It is a town of great trade, and has a good harbour, where there are always many ships, both of those that sail for Sofala, and those that come from Cambay in India and Malindi, and others which sail to the islands of Zanzibar, Mafia, and Pemba, which will be spoken of further on. This Mombaça is a country well supplied with plenty of food. Here are found very fine sheep, which have round tails, and many cows, chickens, and very large goats, much rice, and millet, and plenty of oranges, sweet and bitter, and lemons, limes, pomegranates, Indian figs and all sorts of vegetables, and very good water.

These tall white houses strung out along the coast beside the sparkling sea, with their foreign trade, harbours, and all the evidence of prosperity, were a source of wonder and amazement to the Portuguese. And still the towns remained separate states, often at enmity with each other, and each one with its own trading ventures. It seems that they never became united and even when the Portuguese later attacked them, they did not join together to resist a common enemy.

A mosque on the Red Sea coast.

Beyond the fact that the interests of these cities were linked by a common purpose in the same prosperous trading activities, they were also linked by having the same culture and the same language. Their language was Swahili – from the Arabic word meaning 'the coast' – and although it has many Arabic words, it is basically an African language having the same grammar as those of the Bantu family. It differs from other Bantu languages only in the unusually large number of words borrowed from other tongues – a reflexion of the number of foreigners who visited the coast; as well as those from Arabic, words from Portuguese, Turkish, Indian, Malay, Persian, German, and English can all be distinguished in modern Swahili, though the latter two languages must have made their contribution comparatively lately. Swahili was written down until very recent times in the Arabic script, (which is occasionally still used) and literature, poetry as well as prose, survives from about the eighteenth century onwards. The poems of the Swahili writers were famous and tell us much about the life and times of the poets, so that they are of considerable value to historians.

The arrival of the Portuguese along the coast was disastrous to the prosperous, easy-going civilization which had become established there. The Portuguese were energetic and well-armed, and as they came to understand the extent and wealth of the Indian Ocean trade, they were filled with a determination to control it, to have access to the riches of the countries involved in it, and to acquire such loot as they could while so doing. They fell upon the towns of the East Coast with a cruelty and ferocity which the coastal people were unable to resist with their own lack of unity and feebler weapons. Their intention was to subdue the coastal towns and use them as a base for attacking countries further east. The first city to suffer a Portuguese attack was Mozambique, and in the years closely following A.D. 1500, Kilwa was forced to pay tribute to the King of Portugal and was later sacked and burnt. When the Portuguese fleet entered the port of Kilwa, according to the report of Vasco da Gama, all the people felt great fear because they had heard of the 'events of Mozambique and Malindi'. They agreed to trade and live in friendship with the Portuguese, but this was not enough; the Portuguese demanded tribute, as a token of friendship, 'of a certain sum of money, or a rich jewel' to be paid each year to their King. This made the Sultan of Kilwa very sad, for he said that such friendship with the enforced paying of tribute was dishonourable, and had he guessed that such was the intention of the King of Portugal, he would have fled to the woods 'for it is better to be a jackal at large, than a greyhound bound with a golden leash'. Eventually he was forced to pay tribute however, to save his town and his people from being burnt, but even this did not prevent its ultimate destruction. Mombasa and many other fair and peaceful towns, with years of history behind them and great traditions of trade, were destroyed and their citizens massacred. The towns were seized; the trade routes altered to suit the new rulers; and later great forts, like Fort Jesus at Mombasa, were built to house garrisons to control the local populations.

During the 200 years in which the Portuguese controlled the east coast trade, it never recovered its former state. This was partly because they deliberately disorganized the old and tested trade routes in order to benefit towns further south where their foothold on Africa was more firmly established – ships sailed from Goa, the Portuguese capital in India, to Mozambique, instead of

A Portuguese fort at Lamu built in the sixteenth century. (*From Elspeth Huxley: 'The Sorcerer's Apprentice' Chatto & Windus.*)

from Cambay, in India, to Malindi, Kilwa and other ports. Apart from this disruption, they used the towns rather as bases for organizing trade than as trading centres, and one of the reasons for this was that they had comparatively little to export. They never understood that the Arabs, while they lived on the coast and organized their business in the ports, were yet dependent on caravans which they sent inland for supplies of gold, ivory and all the other goods which they needed for export. Moreover they never won the goodwill of the people. So trade declined, and the towns grew poorer and weaker, so much so that attacks on them by another African people, the Zimba, were successful, and they took Kilwa and Mombasa from the Portuguese, and sacked them.

In spite of all the growing poverty and weakened trade, Swahili culture did not disappear, and after the decay of Portuguese power in the seventeenth century, there was some revival in many of the towns, and some of the old spirit came back. It is in this period from the late seventeenth century to the end of the eighteenth that we have the fullest information about the Swahili towns, and of their political history, social organization, and the manners and customs of the people. The little states, each one controlling its own territory in the immediate neighbourhood, continued to be ruled by kings, as had always been their custom, but now real power seems to have fallen into the hands of a class of aristocrats. They were probably the wealthy people who encouraged and supported the poets of this time, whose poetry tells us much of city life and the behaviour of the ruling classes. The most famous of these is a long religious poem called 'Al-Inkishafi', which gives a detailed description of towns which have been lost and forgotten. One of these, Kua, in the Mafia Islands off the coast, had for long been unvisited until the poet's words led people to go and look for it. The place was buried in dense bush, but once this had been hacked away, the site of the town was easily seen, and ruins of fine houses of the late eighteenth century were found. There were palaces, the houses of noble men, decorated elaborately, and the walls of the rooms were lined with little niches for the display of precious pottery and porcelain. Kua was destroyed by Madagascan pirates in 1790. Many other towns lie in ruins, known or as yet undiscovered, hidden under bush and sand. They could tell us much about the elegant and settled civilization which the poets describe. One of them wrote of Pate, another of the great coastal towns:

> Nyumba kati zao huvuma mende;
> Kumbi za msana hulia ngende.

> The cockroach whirring flits the empty halls;
> Where nobles gathered, shrill the cricket calls.

Those things which remain to us of the culture of the coast, the writings, ruined buildings, the broken Chinese pottery and other remnants of trade, are, in the main, evidence of the settlement of foreigners in the various towns, for they are mostly Arab in inspiration. The coastal people were much affected by Arab ways and adopted their dress, became Muslims, built mosques and tombs like those of the Arabs, and took many Arabic words into their language, and there is no doubt that the overall impression of this civilization must be that it was heavily influenced by Arab settlers. Yet, though the hold on their own culture must have been almost broken by the weight of foreign influences on them, the local people retained some of their own customs and beliefs steadfastly, fusing them with those of the Arabs and giving the Swahili culture its character. Ibn Battuta, an Arab traveller visiting Kilwa in the fourteenth century, noted some African characteristics among the people, as for example their custom of decorating their faces with cuts, and comments on the difference between their food and that to which he was accustomed, both as to the dishes provided and the amount, which he says was three times as much as he could eat! Elsewhere we can read that each state kept a Great Drum, or Ivory Horn, symbol of the power of the state, which was carefully guarded as a ritual object, an African rather than an Arab custom. Witch doctors are said to have flourished along with Muslim priests, and although the religion of the coast was that of Islam, it was tempered by the local people with their own spirits and beliefs. How deeply the ordinary people were affected by Arab ways, it is difficult to say, but there is no doubt that this coastal civilization affected only the coast, for there is no evidence that the people who lived inland came under its influence in any way, except for necessary trading activities.

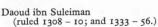

Daoud ibn Suleiman
(ruled 1308 – 10; and 1333 – 56.)

Ali ibn el Hassan (ruled 1478 – 79.)

Some of the Sultans (kings) of Kilwa minted their own coins, and these are examples of them. They are all copper coins, and each bears the name of the Sultan who minted it, in Arabic script. They are all of the fourteenth and fifteenth centuries.

113

8. The Stone Citadel of Zimbabwe

WHEN the ruins of Zimbabwe were first made known to the world, they were regarded as a great mystery, and there must have been as many theories about their purpose and origin as there were visitors to them. They were first brought to attention in recent times in 1868, by a European hunter who was wandering in the bush, and at that time they were quite overgrown with creepers and were not easy to see. Later visitors made a greater study of the ruins and were much impressed by their size and grandeur, and a variety of original ideas were put about as to who might have built such great walls and towers. Once traces of ancient gold workings were discovered in the neighbourhood, people flocked there in search of gold, ransacking the ruins, and destroying evidence which would have been helpful to later scientific investigators who were anxious to find out the history of the place. A company called 'The Ancient Ruins Company Limited' was formed by two Europeans whose object was to 'exploit all the ancient ruins south of the Zambesi River', but in fact their real purpose was to find such loot as they could by exploring all the known ruins. The Company only lasted five years, from 1895 to 1900, when it was ordered to be closed down but it did much damage in that time; two years later, a law was passed which forbade such destruction of ancient buildings and objects. Later, in 1905, the first scientific archaeological examination of the ruins was made, and after that, in 1929, a second archaeologist confirmed the opinions of the first, namely that all the evidence showed 'not one single item that was not in accordance with the claim of Bantu origin and mediaeval date', and that while some of the buildings might have been made as copies of things heard of, or seen, on the East African coast, there was no doubt that the builders were Africans. More recent archaeological work and scientific tests carried out on objects found there have confirmed this opinion, and have told us more about the date of the buildings; and so, to a great extent, the early mystery has been solved.

As you will see from the map, Zimbabwe lies in the centre of Southern Rhodesia. There are two main groups of ruins; one, known as the 'Acropolis', crowns a hill where there is an outcrop of granite rocks and boulders, and might well have been a hill fort; the other lies about a quarter of a mile south of the Acropolis and is often called the 'Temple' ruins. The 'Temple' is the site which caught people's imagination so strongly, for it lies in a gentle wooded valley, and is surrounded by a massive wall enclosing an oval area about 300 feet long and 200 feet across. Inside the wall is a second wall and other buildings, including a solid conical tower to which nothing exactly similar has been seen anywhere else in the world. Between these two main groups, lie the 'Valley Ruins', a mass of broken walls and small stone enclosures, where it is thought the majority of the inhabitants of Zimbabwe lived. All these buildings are made of slabs of stone, fitted together without any mortar to hold them in place. They have been cut from the 'leaves' of granite, which is plentiful in this area, and which time cracks off in flat, manageable pieces from the parent rock. This type of building is quite distinctive, for the stones are skilfully matched together till they sit firmly, and sometimes are even laid in patterns for decoration to a building. The huge wall which encloses the 'Temple' is a great feat of building – it still stands 30 feet high – and is so thick and massive that a very great deal of

The medieval stone ruins in modern Rhodesia.

115

Aerial view of the temple at Great Zimbabwe. A section of the valley of ruins may be seen in the left background. (*Government of Southern Rhodesia.*)

time and labour must have been spent in the building of it. There is no sign that the buildings were roofed with anything other than thatch and a kind of rough cement made from anthills which had been pounded to a powder. On the 'Acropolis', clever use was made of the granite boulders which cover the hill naturally, for they were joined together by stone walls into a defensive system. In general, the style of building is a simple one – the walls usually enclose a circular space, entrances are rounded and in fact the buildings must have looked much like the circular houses made of mud or cane with thatched roofs, which are common in places where stone is not so easily available.

We assume the Acropolis was a fortress meant to defend the buildings below in the valley from attack, and the buildings within the great oval wall, the so-called Temple, were probably the palace of the chief. Within the maze of walls and passages lived the chief, protected from the eyes of the ordinary people. His house was circular, and nearby a special platform was found on which stood a number of upright stones (or monoliths) which may have been the place where he held his court and gave audience to his people. The houses of his wives and court officials would also have been within this enclosure. Outside in the Valley Ruins lived the ordinary people, no doubt with enclosures for their cattle which would feed on the pasture of the hillsides, where also some cultivation of crops would be organized. In times of danger or attack, the whole population probably took flight to the Acropolis for protection, returning to their homes only when it was safe to do so again.

It is now known from scientific investigation, that the ruins were not all built at the same time, and that there has been much re-building. The earliest buildings are considered to have been made at a time not earlier than the eleventh century A.D., and to have been in use until the fifteenth century; while the later buildings, amongst which are the great oval wall and the conical tower, are now known to belong to a later period, dating from the seventeenth and early eighteenth centuries.

The history of the earlier period at Zimbabwe is not known with any certainty, for we do not hear of Zimbabwe in any written works before the arrival of the Portuguese on the East coast in the early sixteenth century. By that time, the original inhabitants of Zimbabwe had moved northwards, but they remembered their first home in their tribal stories, and some information has come to us.

Animals carved on soapstone bowls found at Zimbabwe. *Below:* Statue of a bird made of soapstone, one of several found standing on upright columns.

When the Portuguese reached Sofala, famous for its trade in gold, it did not take them long to discover that the gold came from inland. They took control of Sofala, and would like to have been able to reach the source of the supply of gold and control that too, but this was more of an undertaking. However, they soon found out that the most powerful of the suppliers of gold were a people called the Karanga, who were ruled by a chief known as the Mwenemutapa, or as the Portuguese wrote it, the Monomatapa. These were the people who had lived at Zimbabwe, and they remembered their old home, not personally but in their peoples' traditional stories, and they said that they had moved away because supplies of salt became scarce. The Portuguese met them or heard gossip about them on the coast, and from Portuguese writings, and archaeological evidence, we can learn something about them, remembering always that this is how they were after they had moved from Zimbabwe, for we have no information of their life there, though we may safely assume that their manner of life and customs would not have changed greatly.

In 1517, Barbosa, a Portuguese writer, wrote from Mozambique, 'Beyond this country towards the interior lies the great kingdom of Monomatapa', and we find that it was considered the leader of all the kingdoms of the inland area. The people were dark-skinned and came down to Sofala to sell or exchange their gold and ivory. Some, says Barbosa, 'go naked except from the waist down', while the most noble wore capes of skins with tassels of tails which trailed along the ground as a mark of dignity and importance, and 'carried swords thrust into wooden scabbards, bound with much gold and other metals, worn on the left side . . . They also carry assegais in their hands, and others carry bows and arrows of middle size. The iron arrowheads are long and finely pointed. They are warlike men and some too are great traders.' It was said that the Monomatapa's people carried their gold to the coast and sold it without weighing it, taking in return coloured cloths and silks and beads which they valued highly. We have seen, in the last chapter, the wealth of the coastal trade, and a fair proportion of that must have been based on the gold which the Karanga people and others in the interior produced. At the height of its greatness, perhaps in the thirteenth and fourteenth centuries, Zimbabwe must have been a wealthy place. In the sixteenth century, we know from the Portuguese, that the Karanga were distinguished from

118

the others of the region because they wore cloth, which they could well afford.

Of their state organization, we can also learn something from the Portuguese sixteenth-century writers. It is clear that the Monomatapa was not just a ruler or chief; he was also regarded as being divine, the sort of god-king whom we have seen in other of the African kingdoms. His people approached him crawling on their stomachs, and were not allowed to look at him, and at audiences, they merely heard his voice speaking to them from behind a curtain or screen. The king's every action was imitated by his courtiers, so that if he coughed, they all coughed too; if he drank, they all drank. He was expected to be in excellent health and without any physical disability such as deafness, or any other bodily failing, so that as he flourished in good health, the state should grow strong with him. When he became old or ill he was expected to take poison, so that, for the well-being of his kingdom, a younger or healthier man should take his place and the state should not grow ill and weak in company with its old ruler. When the king died, his spirit was thought to enter into a lion, which for this reason was regarded as a sacred animal and might not be killed except at a hunt in the presence of the ruling king. The king was often referred to as The Lion.

At court, everything was highly organized. There was a number of official posts to be held; chancellor of the kingdom, court chamberlain, military commander, keeper of the sacred tribal relics, head drummer, head cook, head doorkeeper and others, and the title passed from one holder of office to the next. The queen mother and the nine official wives of the king each had her own small court and officials within the palace enclosure, and there were about 3000 serving women also living there. Away from the court, subject kings and province governors all lived in a less grand but similar way, and were expected to send their sons to the Monomatapa's court to become pages in his service, or warriors. An important symbol of the king, and therefore of the welfare of the kingdom, was the royal fire, which burned as long as the king lived. Subject states and all the chiefs within the kingdom lit their own fires from the royal fire, and once a year, after ceremonies in May, these fires had to be kindled anew as a mark of allegiance to the king. Messengers set out carrying torches set alight in the royal fire, each to his own chief, and the accepting of the fire was

Iron tools found at Zimbabwe. Above is an ingot which may have been used as money; underneath is a hoe. (*British Museum.*)

the symbol of the chief's acceptance of the Monomatapa as his great ruler. When the king died, all the fires in the country were put out, to be set alight once again when the new ruler came to his throne.

Archaeological excavation has shown us many of the things which were in use at Zimbabwe. Amongst them are pottery, iron arrow heads and spears, parts of hoes, and much gold work. There were also found some statues of birds made of soapstone, each bird standing on an upright column. These are thought to have had a ceremonial use and, being found in the Temple, probably were the work of the people who rebuilt much of that enclosure after the Monomatapa had left, but they have become famous, and should be noticed here. Other things found were goods brought up from the coast, such as fragments of Chinese porcelain, Persian pottery, Arab glass, Indian and Indonesian beads. These show not only that the people of Zimbabwe were in touch with foreigners for trading purposes, but are helpful in trying to date the things belonging to Zimbabwe, for the dates at which some of the imports were made can be fixed fairly accurately.

It is not clear whether the Monomatapa left Zimbabwe entirely of his own free will, because, as the traditional story says, salt supplies had run out, or whether he was driven out by the Rozwi, who took over Zimbabwe in about the sixteenth century. The Rozwi were strong, and their ruler, the Mambo, took possession of most of the old Monomatapa kingdom, establishing himself as the new ruler. They stayed there until 1834, when the last Mambo was killed by invading Zulu, and the kingdom destroyed. In the meantime, however, the Rozwi became powerful, and were threatening the new home of the Monomatapa – so much so, in fact, that in 1629, the Monomatapa tried to get help from the Portuguese against the Mambo and his people. In this way, the Monomatapa lost his independence, becoming a subject state owing allegiance to the Portuguese overlords; and it did not in the end help his people, for the kingdom declined and grew weak, and subject kingdoms broke their treaties with the Monomatapa and joined with the Rozwi instead. At last in a series of battles and skirmishes which lasted from 1693 to 1695, the Rozwi drove the Monomatapa and his Portuguese protectors out of their land, and they had to withdraw to a tiny part of their kingdom, powerless, and still subject to the Portuguese.

Iron spear from Khami.

120

The Monomatapa's people, the Karanga, and the Mambo's people, the Rozwi, were different branches of the same people, the Shona, who are Bantu-speaking Africans. Between them, they were responsible for the remarkable ruins at Zimbabwe, and perhaps also for a series of other stone buildings in modern Southern Rhodesia, and the northern part of the Transvaal. Over 300 ruins have been listed, though some of them are quite small. Amongst them, however, are other impressive ruins such as those at Khami, Dhlo-Dhlo, Naletali and Mapungubwe. While none of these is as exciting a ruin as Zimbabwe, they are all built of stone in the same way as Zimbabwe, and are the same type of enclosed township. At Khami, some famous ivory figurines were found; at Naletali, the walls are remarkable for their decoration of patterned stone work; at Mapungubwe, which had never been disturbed by robbers of ancient ruins, a marvellous hoard of gold work was found. 'Gold beads, bangles, and bits of thin gold plating. were found according to a report of the finding of this place, and 'large pieces of plate gold, some of them shaped. These were the remains of little rhinoceroses which had consisted of thin plate gold tacked by means of small gold tacks on to some core of wood or other substance which had perished. Solid gold tails and ears, beautifully made, had likewise been tacked on to these figures" The excavation of these sites opened a window on to a scene in the African past which had previously been hidden from us, and helped to reveal the history of another stretch of Africa. There is still much to be discovered, as is true of many other parts of this continent, but with the patient work of scholars, the outlines and achievements of the past are being sketched in.

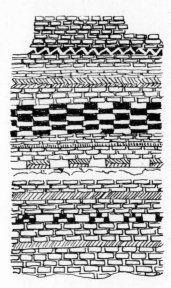

A wall at Naletali showing the complicated patterns used in building. (*After James Walton.*)

Ivory statuette from Khami ruins.

121

A SHORT BIBLIOGRAPHY

The list of books which follows is intended for those who wish to read further.

The first three deal with the whole of Africa; the others are about particular areas. None of these is highly specialized (no reports of archaeological excavation are included, for example) and each one is the result of recent research.

A Short History of Africa, Roland Oliver & J. D. Fage (Penguin Books, 1962).

Old Africa Rediscovered, Basil Davidson (Chatto & Windus, 1959).

The Dawn of African History, ed. Roland Oliver (1961).

A History of the Sudan to 1821, A. J. Arkell (University of London, 1961).

The Golden Trade of the Moors, E. W. Bovill (Oxford University Press, 1958).

Archéologie Tchadienne, J-P. Lebeuf (Paris, 1962).

La Civilisation du Tchad, Lebeuf et Masson Detourbet (Paris, 1950).

A History of Islam in West Africa, J. S. Trimingham (Oxford University Press, 1962).

Introduction to the History of West Africa, J. D. Fage (Cambridge University Press, 1962).

The Northern Factor in Ashanti History, Ivor Wilks (Ghana, 1961).

The Prehistory of East Africa, Sonia Cole (Penguin Books, 1954).

The Prehistory of South Africa, Desmond Clark (Penguin Books, 1959).

The Medieval History of the Coast of Tanganyika, G. S. P. Freeman-Grenville (Oxford University Press, 1962).

History of East Africa, ed. Roland Oliver & Gervase Mathew (Oxford University Press 1963).

Zimbabwe: A Rhodesian Mystery, Roger Summers (Nelson, 1963).

INDEX

DATE DUE

JUL 3 '68		
JUL 1 7 1970		
RESERVE		
APR 1 1 1973		
APR 8 1981		
OCT 2 2 1984 RECD		
APR 1 1 1992		
MAR 3 1 1993		
GAYLORD		PRINTED IN U.S.A.